BUILD THE VISION

ADVANCE TOWARD YOUR OPTIMAL LIFE

Contents

FOREWORD

Like most people, chances are you desire more for your life than you currently have. Be it better relationships, a more fulfilling job, better health or more money. Whatever your heart's desire is, it's not unusual for people to simply want to improve their circumstances. In Nick's book, "Build the Vision: Advance Toward Your Optimal Life," he approaches the Law of Attraction from a user-friendly, actionable standpoint while providing you with the tools necessary to put theory into practice.

After a year of Zoom meetings, phone calls and emails with the author, I've witnessed Nick's research, interviews, and investigations cumulate into an actionable template that can benefit both the expert and the novice. This well-crafted document isn't just another pie-in-the-sky, name it and claim it "Law of Attraction" book. "Build the Vision" offers so much more than that. It provides concrete, actionable, easy-to-follow steps that will accelerate your advance toward living your optimal life—a life you truly deserve.

I suggest you take time to become one with it, embed the content, and follow the instructions. Allow the content to become both a lesson and a lifestyle. If you do that, this body of work will significantly impact your life for the better.

– Dr. D. Ivan Young, MCC, NBC-HWC, CPDC

PREFACE

Welcome. My name is Nick, and I'll be your guide throughout this book.

"Who are you? And why would I listen to you?"

Good question. You're in luck, I'm a straight shooter, so let's get those questions out of the way. Grab a comfy seat because class is in session. Here's a little about me.

Picture this: It's 2013 and I'm right around fourteen years old. The school bell rings obnoxiously, and the hallway transforms from a place of quiet serenity to a deafening, commotion-filled rally. Students walk through halls decorated with pieces of academic achievement, school-spirit posters, and sports memorabilia.

As I pass by the sea of faces, I can't help but annotate *every* anxious feeling and thought that races through my mind. The external world seems blocked as I'm caught up in my internal world of worry. I enter the room of my next class and find a seat.

Frustration sets in. I acknowledge I'm upset that I keep letting my thoughts and emotions get the best of me. I worry and ask myself, *Is this how it will always be?* The worry continues. Eventually, it escalates to overwhelming anxiety.

Throughout my adolescence, when I couldn't find the answer to the said question or others like it, I would be sent into an anxious frenzy that left me feeling like a robot in the midst of an overload. My mind was fuzzy, my body felt awful, and it felt like my entire world was spiraling. I couldn't make sense of anything; it felt as if I was maneuvering through a made-up world; a dream, though not one of my own.

That was me before I took the time to work on myself, long before I knew how to get help or how to articulate to others, or even myself, what was going on. I was anxious; I was nervous; I overthought everything and perpetually overflowed with fears and emotions. I questioned my existence, grew frustrated with things outside of my control, and put too much pressure on myself to do everything perfectly.

These problems controlled me as best they could for some time—until I realized they didn't have to.

It wasn't as simple as flipping a switch or anything like that. It took time and effort, as most good things do. I grew sick of my circumstances, so I took steps in the right direction—looking for ways to fix my problems instead of wondering if they'd go away.

There my journey began in pursuit of an optimal life.

But before I could help myself, I had to acknowledge that I wasn't knowledgeable enough. I simply didn't know enough about myself or the issues I was dealing with. So, I searched for and became more mindful of opportunities to learn more from my experiences and from others.

I looked for answers. These answers would help me understand why I was the way I was and how I could help myself become the person I wanted to be so badly.

My journey wasn't a walk in the park. But while I was trying to become this *optimal* version of myself, I had learned a few tips and tricks that helped me along the way—which are listed in this book.

Thanks to my journey, I had the opportunity to learn many lessons, and I was given plenty of eye-opening experiences that helped shape me into the person I am today. Through this journey, I overcame a major ego issue, learned to let go, and, among many other things, became more empathetic.

"Well, why me? Why should I read this?"

The concepts and tactics we explore in this book are time-tested, backed by research from knowledgeable experts, fact-based articles, and other insightful books. Additionally, I was fortunate to connect with a few extraordinary individuals who assisted me with this book's development.

I've also attached a wellness piece. Wellness can improve your overall quality of life. It's a concept and practice that will assist your mind and body as you take strides toward your optimal life.

Now, don't get it twisted. I'm not a self-help expert, a doctor, or a psychologist. Nor am I perfect; I have my issues like everyone else. I am just a human who has learned a few helpful things throughout my journey toward an optimal life.

These concepts and tactics have worked for me and have assisted those who have so generously taught said concepts and tactics to me. This is the book I would want to give to my younger self, as it would've saved me plenty of time. I hope that it will do that for you.

If you struggle with similar issues to what I've described in my personal story above, there will be something of use here. So, don't waste another minute wishing for someone else to swoop in and save you from the problems in your own life; try some concepts and tactics in this book in real time.

Every second you spend wishing that things were different—complaining about this, worrying about that—you could instead build yourself into the type of person who eats those problems for breakfast.

You can totally maneuver around these obstacles, but it is *your* responsibility to do so. While, in this book, we'll explore practical ways to overcome these obstacles, it falls on you to apply them. I can't emphasize this enough. It is up to you, and only you, to help yourself.

Also, I'm not here to prove something to you or sell you half-baked ideas. I am simply presenting concepts and tactics so you may utilize those that resonate with you to get you closer to where you want to be.

Whether you're dealing with something minor or daunting, there's something in this book for everyone. I suggest reading through with a highlighter, taking time to highlight ideas that speak to you. From there, go out and apply pressure wherever it's needed.

But that's enough of the intro. Let's see what this book is all about. With that, I present *Build the Vision: Advance Toward Your Optimal Life*.

Enjoy.

PART I — VISION

If you've been living under a rock, here's an interesting fact—life is not perfect.

And neither are we. That's right; we're not perfect. Sorry to burst your bubble, but we're flawed beings. Yes, that includes you and everyone you know too.

Perfection is a make-believe concept that holds us back. We are humans. We are ever-changing beings. In our lives, things constantly move, rearrange, and evolve. What seems perfect to us today may not be tomorrow. What is perfect to one person may not be to another. So, if we attempt to pursue perfection, we will find that the search never ends.

So, retire the idea of perfection. Expectations of perfection are unrealistic and will ultimately lead to disappointment as your idea of perfection may alter or require additional add-ons to keep you content. With that said, while we create our vision, we aim to design an optimal life, not a perfect one. While that distinction may seem subtle, it's very important.

The reason we're looking to design an optimal life is so we can develop an actual "game plan" and identify attainable goals. This way we can make real progress toward becoming the person we want to become.

Contrary to popular belief, it is 100% possible to change our lives. All it takes is some effort and direction. When we adjust our daily habits, lifestyle, thought process, and attitude, we will notice *real* changes in our lives.

But this won't come easy. I don't want to mislead you—while creating your optimal life and taking steps toward becoming the person you want to be is invigorating, the process is undoubtedly difficult. It takes commitment, dedication, and discipline.

Let's be honest. If it was easy, everyone would do it. Implementing change into your life requires a process. It requires a process of trial and error, which comes with frustration, disappointment, satisfaction, and happiness—and everything between.

You may go to hell and back, but it won't matter because when you look back, you'll be so grateful for how far you've come—so damn happy that you are out of that awful place you started in.

But none of that will matter unless you're willing to go through this roller coaster of a process. And that process, my friend, is for you and you alone. It is a solo venture, not for the faint of heart.

So, if you're up for the challenge and this sounds like something you're ready for, we can get started.

Let's jump in, shall we?

First, we must create a vision.

Our vision is what will help keep us on track as it provides a sense of *direction*. Once we have our vision, we can make strides toward our optimal life on a clearer and more defined path. But, before we create the vision for our optimal life, let's talk about an extraordinary tool we can utilize to shape our vision: perspective.

CHAPTER 1: PERSPECTIVE

Our perspective is the window that connects us to the world. It's like our own personal news channel that delivers information to our brains. Every individual has a perspective shaped by their personal experiences, mind-state, values, morals, etc.

A genuine perspective is vital to our vision. We must become mindful in this area to ensure our vision isn't tainted with outside influences telling us how our life "should" be. Instead, let's question our current methods and check in with ourselves to make sure our decisions are our own and not the byproduct of someone else's ideas.

Now, there will be a handful of perspectives you may agree with or gravitate toward and adopt. This is normal.

Not everything is an original idea—obviously. Almost everything we do or like is derived from someone or somewhere else. Most of these perspectives, ideas, and interests, if not all, were not invented by us. Although, they influence us the most.

All ideas and concepts that exist were created by someone no different than you, and your perspective of a particular topic is not skewed if learned from elsewhere if it aligns with your true self. Essentially, what I am saying is that we must do our own research. Our perspective must align with our true self and should not derive from somewhere else without firsthand examination.

When we take another's word at face value without taking time to educate ourselves, we adopt a perspective filled with ideas, values, and morals we may disagree with. If we act on the perspectives, we will ultimately be dissatisfied with the outcomes they provide and have wasted our time and energy looking through a lens that isn't our own.

There are two ways we can use our perspective: authentically and inauthentically. Now, what does this mean? This means we either observe, distinguish, and evaluate information based on our opinions, inferences, and ideas or allow outside influences to do this for us.

If we're using our perspective authentically, we're thinking for ourselves. When using our perspective inauthentically, we're letting other people's opinions, inferences, and ideas have power over our own. We're letting others think for us.

Therefore, we should be cautious when shaping our personal perspectives.

Now, there's no right or wrong way to use a perspective. It's our viewpoint dictated by us. But that's my point—you must shape your perspective, and you must do so alone. Formulate your own ideas, frame situations according to you, and come to your own conclusions.

Think for yourself and follow your moral compass on your journey as you advance toward your vision.

LIGHT IN THE DARK

Your perspective determines your world.

Your outlook stems from your personal narrative. And the personal narrative you're creating isn't a byproduct of simply your experiences but of your relationship with those experiences.

More simply, your reality is determined by how you think about everything you've experienced in life, not by the experiences themselves.

You see, it all ties back to perspective: how we perceive our life experiences is *crucial.* Deliberate for your own sake and don't let preconceived ideas disrupt your authentic perspective.

So, question everything. Don't let someone else's reality become your own simply because you didn't take the time to formulate and examine your own opinions, inferences, or ideas.

If we take on perspectives that aren't precisely ours, they will lead us in unwanted directions heading to unwanted destinations. We cannot let outside perspectives alter our own.

We do not need outside validation to craft our own perspectives. Think for yourself and allow your perspective to assist you in your endeavors.

Generally, we want to set ourselves up to make the best of any situation that comes our way. We want to make our perspectives work for us, not against us.

"So, how can we do that?"

We can have our perspectives work for us by prompting a particular desired outcome from any situation, whether the situation is good or bad. We do this by reframing our perspective of our problems so we may benefit from them. This concept is about finding *light in the dark*—the good in the bad.

Here, I'll explain.

As humans, a lot of us are obsessed with one thing: ourselves. That's right; we're submerged into a deep pool of our own self-importance. And, ironically, it's bringing us down.

Often, as humans, we're egotistical and overly self-absorbed. We think we're the most extraordinary thing on the planet, and not one bad thing should happen to a single hair on our perfect little head. And if you're one of these people, brace yourself for the following statement.

We're not that special.

Truth be told, many of our problems become amplified by the frustration of dealing with adversity. It's as if we believe that we're too "special" to deal with problems. When said problems crop up, we act in disbelief. We can't wrap our heads around the idea that something rotten could *actually* happen to us.

These situations often breed resentment, which may be a reason for the lack of action we take to fix said problems when they arise. Essentially, we feel like these problems shouldn't be ours to deal with. We act as if there's been some sort of mistake.

Listen, if you haven't figured it out by now, not everything is sunshine and rainbows all of the time. You're not "above" dealing with problems, and you're not "too special" for problems. Sometimes, shit happens.

"What's your point?"

Life isn't always going to go your way—and that's okay. We can't control everything. We can barely control anything—only a few things, really. And, when we conclude that not everything is in our control, we will eliminate 90% of our problems.

We have a preconceived idea that problems are an inconvenient and imperfect blemish on the face of our perfect lives. Once we understand that this idea is inaccurate, we can stop it from bringing us down. But first, we must learn to accept that problems are a part of life and not a shortcoming. The sooner we realize this, the better off we'll be.

Only when we conclude this may we begin to reframe our perspective of our problems so they can benefit us. We can't find light in the dark if every problem is inconvenient or catastrophic. We must shift our perspective to understand that problems are incognito opportunities.

Believe it or not, every problem is embedded with an opportunity for growth. When new problems appear, it may help to ponder the issue at hand and ask yourself: What is this trying to teach me?

Before you attack the problem head-on, consider what you may learn from it; search for a potential lesson you may have overlooked. If your boss hands you a rather large and important project at work, understand that it's an opportunity and not an overwhelming project to get worked up about.

You're being presented with an opportunity to work on a project of a much higher caliber than you traditionally would. Recognize this as a chance to challenge yourself. It's an opportunity to show yourself and others what you're capable of. Accept it as such.

Put your head down and work. Next thing you know, you've solved your "problem" and have something to show for it too: a well-done project and a new personal lesson or piece of information.

Each time we solve a problem, it's an opportunity to learn another helpful lesson or piece of information. We must seize these opportunities to protect ourselves for the next time something similar occurs.

When we become mindful of these opportunities and prompt ourselves to learn from these experiences, only then may we grow.

If we're able to rethink our perspective of adversity and view our problems as opportunities, we can turn moments of grief and frustration into those of satisfaction and joy—all while obtaining lessons and information as we continue to grow.

CHAPTER 2: EXPECTATIONS

Expectations are a silent killer.

Theodore Roosevelt once said, "Comparison is the thief of joy."[1] When we find ourselves disappointed with an experience, it is always tied to our own expectations of the experience. We compare the reality of an outcome to a preconceived idea that we created.

Our expectations derive from preconceived ideas around long before we were even born. That's right—most of these expectations don't even stem from us. Most of the time, unconsciously, we create these expectations ourselves from bits of information from outside sources. This collection of information fuses to form one enormous assumption.

We create expectations when we take in too many outside perspectives, preconceived ideas, and pieces of information instead of considering our own perspectives. These expectations are, at their core, utter nonsense.

"How so?"

A lot of the expectations we have for ourselves are not designed by us directly, even though sometimes we think they are. Most of the time, without even realizing it, the expectations we have for ourselves are designed by others and spoon-fed to us without warning. And if we step out of line with others' expectations, they will tell us to be "more realistic" or "come down to Earth."

Some of us believe that the expectations given to us, whether by a parent, friend, teacher or whomever, are the only true expectations. This leaves us stranded with our "own" shallow perceptions. And some of us, unfortunately, never learn that many expectations we are accustomed to aren't even necessarily ours.

In his extraordinary book, *The Four Agreements*, Don Miguel Ruiz explores a so-called "societal dream." He argues that long before we were even born, humans had created a world all their own: a "collective dream" made up of billions of other smaller dreams.[2]

This dream includes all of society's laws, rules, beliefs, cultures, etc. All members of society are introduced to these ideas. Even you. Yes, you. As a child, these ideas were presented to you, and you tacitly agreed to them because you knew no better.

Yes, they're your agreements—as of now. But remember, these were not our intentional choices. These agreements were here before we were even born. And as we age, it becomes harder to break the cycle and look beyond these agreements; this is because we rarely realize that we can do so. So, we unknowingly keep ourselves in a box.

This artificial belief system controls our whole life. There are concepts within life that bring definitions to subjective things. For example, we have societal ideas of what a man or woman is—how they should act, what they should do, etc. Because of this system, we learn to judge. We become domesticated through these beliefs.

We give in to the demands that society creates. We have close friends and family who run with these beliefs and agreements. And because we don't want to be the black sheep, be rejected, or be viewed as inadequate, we act. We portray a character we're not and slowly become another copy.[3]

"What are you getting at?"

Plenty of our issues stem from this preconceived belief system we never even agreed to. We're put into situations with overwhelmingly high expectations that derive from artificial perspectives and ideas.

This belief system was made up by other humans and considered an objective way of life that everyone must adopt. Over time, these artificial perspectives and ideas—expectations—are pushed increasingly higher thanks to overexposure from things like social media.

So, this high expectation bullshit is simply an accelerated version of what it once was. And it continues to accelerate each day; the societal expectation level is at an all-time high. No wonder we're stressed 24/7— as time goes on, we're trying to keep up and conform to increasingly higher and more unrealistic expectations.

"I'm not strong enough." "I'm not pretty enough." "I'm not smart enough." These are all examples of the things we may say to ourselves when we don't live up to this impossible norm. It's all the same—a continuous cycle of bullshit lies that society makes us tell ourselves.

Here's the key point: *expectations are destroying your reality.*

Expectations are too damn high, and it's a real problem. Unrealistic expectations add unnecessary stress and warp your view on success. Success varies from person to person. We're all different individuals with different perspectives and goals. How could success be so narrowly defined? There is no textbook way to succeed—that part is up to you.

Becoming mindful of this artificial belief system and understanding it is flawed will help eliminate any stressful scenarios it may cause. You must make strides toward your own definition of success without internalizing the expectations that accompany society's current definition of success.

"How do we do such a thing?"

Well, I pose a solution for you: lower your expectations.

"But if I lower my expectations, how will I amount to anything?"

When you have expectations, you expect something will go a particular way. This is a dangerous way of thinking. We are foolishly developing a make-believe script, and when something is off or someone acts out of character, we're allowing ourselves to become upset as the events didn't unfold as planned.

Expectations set you up for disappointment. Even in predictable environments, things can change. You must prepare for that, and the only way to do so is to know that nothing is constant except change itself.

Regardless of expectation level, with effort and commitment, you will amount to something in one or perhaps even a few areas of your life. It gets a little iffy when you expect things to be exceptional in *every* aspect of life.

In all of your endeavors, learn to take things as they come. Accept them for what they are and embrace these moments, as they will not last forever. Accept the natural unfolding of life; it's all going according to plan. Take a moment to learn from your experiences and use that information to move forward.

Now, while lowering our expectations will help lure us away from potentially disappointing experiences, another tactic *must* be implemented to help us become the best version of ourselves and step closer to our vision.

So, while we lower our expectations, we must also *raise our standards.*

Unlike expectations, which are mere wishes of how you're hoping something will turn out, your standards are what you're actually settling for. In life, nothing comes easy. And if there's something you genuinely want, you will be willing to work for it.

Decide what you want and go for it. *Never settle for anything less than what you want.* Don't just hope for it; work for it. We're all capable of being great, but this only comes with effort.

Reframe your expectations. Do your best to make the best of every situation. When something is shitty, like an experience, call it like it is and accept it. Find the best in what's left of the problem, learn from it, and move forward.

You will grow from these experiences and create a more robust version of your current self. One step at a time, you will become a better version of yourself—a version you can be proud of according to you and only you.

Whether you believe it or not, we control our internal experiences. It's all we truly control. We have no say over what happens externally, though we can respond to them in our own way, internally. Once you realize this, you'll notice you can choose your responses to life's curveballs.

Learn to shift your mindset into a lane that you're proud to call your own.

Acknowledge that it is possible to live life on your terms by responding to life's obstacles the way you want to. View everything through *your* lens.

The world is yours, if and only if you can recognize this.

When we understand the power of perspective and how to make ours work for us, we can aim our mindset in the direction we wish to travel. As you evolve, change your mindset to learn and grow. Ultimately, this is how we take steps toward our vision.

After creating our genuine perspective, we will be one step closer to our vision as this new perspective replaces distracting outside influence with clarity.

DESIGN IT

Our visions are not final destinations. They are simply spots where we can spend time and catch a breather on this ever-changing journey we call life. Remember, things are constantly moving and rearranging—this includes us.

We are ever-evolving human beings with various wants and needs that fluctuate based on our current circumstances. So, if we attach to one particular process, outcome, or desire, we may find ourselves disappointed if that exact expectation is not fulfilled.

Nothing remains the same, and the only constant is change. So, if we can learn to adapt to change, we can more easily overcome the dramatic or overwhelming changes that occur in our lives occasionally.

Life is about the journey, not the destination.

Our destination is a great place to rest between moments of transition and periods of growth. But we will need to adjust again at some point. The point is to learn *how to adjust*, no matter what stands in our way.

Life is about learning how to build your vision and progress toward it with a sense of direction and self-confidence. If we can learn to do such a thing, we're bound to be happier and more prosperous.

Now that you've got a little perspective, you can design an optimal life for yourself. So, after some consideration, tell me, what does this life look like?

Close your eyes and see it. Visualize it, feel it, be there. What does it look like, what does it feel like, and who is around? Are you envisioning peace?

Or maybe it's confidence. Is it that new job you've been wanting? Are you living somewhere new? What actions are you taking?

You should think about your goals and what you're looking to attain, but, more importantly, focus on the type of person you want to become. Consider what characteristics you would need that could help you reach your goals.

So, visualize this new version of yourself. Are you committed, passionate, creative? Are you more loving? Maybe you're more relaxed or optimistic.

Spend some time with yourself and create your vision. Once you've got one locked down, we can take a deeper dive into some concepts and tactics bound to help you on your journey toward your optimal life.

For now, make a quiet promise to yourself to consider and approach each concept and tactic with an open mind. Be prepared to give each one a try to find which ones work best for you.

CHAPTER 3: LAW OF ATTRACTION

A major piece of the puzzle in creating your vision is utilizing the *law of attraction*. This law is for attracting what you want into your life, including opportunities that will help you step closer toward your vision.

"Whoa, slow down. What's the law of attraction?"

Don't worry, I'll explain.

The law of attraction suggests that whatever you give your focus and energy to is what will come back to you. It advocates for the idea that positive thoughts and actions bring positive outcomes, while negative thoughts and actions bring negative outcomes.

Your thoughts act as a magnet for whatever it is you're thinking about. Your thoughts affect what you pay attention to or recognize in your day-to-day life, which helps you attract certain things into your life.

In life, we are all susceptible to the laws of the universe, including the law of attraction. This law is about using our mind to translate whatever it is we're focusing on and materialize it into reality, as long as the *recognition* and *action* steps are present. These two steps are key to utilizing the law of attraction—we'll get to those steps soon enough.

Before diving in too deep, let's nip this familiar issue at the source. There are plenty of preconceived notions about the law of attraction you might have heard. It's not unusual to have heard this concept is hippie-dippie or just plain foolish, but it's genuinely science-backed.

It's also likely that whoever is spewing their negative opinions about this law, saying it's bullshit or doesn't work, is most likely not informed enough about the idea—which typically goes without saying.

Listen here. I will not sit here and tell you that the law of attraction is a magical way of attaining your goals, okay? This isn't a damn fairytale. But it works.

Most people have a problem with the law of attraction because they're under the impression that all you're doing is sitting around, wishing and hoping for stuff to happen or for something to come into your life, and then, boom, it works. However, this is not at all how this law behaves. This law is a practical way of helping you achieve your goals.

While thinking about your goals, hopes, and dreams will help you understand what you want or need to achieve, you must take *action* to help sprout your ideas to fruition. We cannot sit there and "wish" for things. I mean, we can, but by no means is that a considerable strategy.

It's called a law for a reason. It works as such. This law is like the law of gravity; similarly, it abides by principles and rules. The law of attraction suggests that similar things are attracted to one another. But it goes much deeper than that.

Like attracts like, meaning things with similar energy are attracted to one another. Energy is prominent in our lives. *Everything* is made of energy. Yes, everything. People, dogs, oceans, trees, food; anything you can think of has energy.[1]

As humans, we live in what's called an "ocean of motion." Everything you see consists of small molecules that vibrate. And *everything* has a different rate of vibrational frequency. This is known as the law of vibration.[2]

All right, quick pause. Let's do a brief check-in. We've noted that everything is energy and everything has a vibrational frequency. Still with me? Okay, good. Let's continue.

Our bodies are molecular structures. They're masses of energy vibrating at high speed. As humans, we're capable of changing the vibrational frequency that our bodies are experiencing. Did you know that the thoughts in our subconscious mind are what control the vibrational frequency that our bodies inhabit? Well, they do!

Our subconscious thoughts trigger the high or low vibrational frequency that our bodies are in—and it is the quality of these subconscious thoughts that emit different vibrations. Positive subconscious thoughts signal good vibrations (high vibrational frequency), and negative subconscious thoughts signal bad vibrations (low vibrational frequency).[3] And before you say anything, the answer is yes—those damn hippies were right.

The sensations and feelings we have result directly from our body's current vibration. The vibrational frequency we're in can physically affect us in numerous different ways.

Good vibrations bring positive outcomes and results. This is considered a *high frequency*, which brings us joy, peace, and positive feelings and outlooks.

Bad vibrations bring negative outcomes and results. This is considered a *low frequency*, which has the opposite effect of a high frequency, leaving us feeling down and sad.[4]

Consider this: The subconscious mind stores our past experiences, memories, and thoughts. It has plenty to do with our habits, recurring ideas, and beliefs. Evidently, with consistency and mental conditioning, the quality of thoughts in our conscious mind can heavily influence the state of our subconscious mind.[5]

And remember, the subconscious mind is what can set off a signal to change your body's vibration, ultimately changing how you're feeling.

We can think positive thoughts all we want in our conscious mind, but the aim is to *influence* our subconscious mind—which is mentally conditioned for a specific type of thinking. So, again, with consistency and mental conditioning, we can use our conscious mind to impress a specific thought quality into our subconscious.

So, it's vital we fill our conscious mind with positivity and the thoughts we want to have regularly, as the habit of positive thinking is then relayed to our subconscious. One way we can do this is through affirmations (which we will get to later). After some time, the conscious thoughts we choose will eventually slide into our unconscious thoughts—which, again, alters the vibration our body inhabits.[6]

Aside from the quality of our thoughts, other ways to improve our frequency include practicing gratitude, meditation, and eating healthy.[7]

Ultimately, our vibrational frequency affects how we feel *and* view everything.

The way we feel and view things will alter our actions, which alter our habits, our choices, who we choose to be around, how we act, and how we operate; the way we feel and view things decides *how we live our lives*.

Here's a summary of what's above:

- Conscious thoughts affect your subconscious thoughts.
- Subconscious thoughts affect your frequency.
- Frequency affects your feelings and viewpoints.
- Feelings and viewpoints affect your actions.
- Actions affect everything else in your life.

Let's bring this full circle. Back to the primary idea here, which is that *like attracts like*. Plain and simple. But why is this important?

When you're marching toward a goal, desire, or vision, you need to be attracting things that will assist you along the way while simultaneously getting rid of things that hold you back.

Some people may not be in the same frequency as you; maybe they say things that make you doubt yourself. Some places may not be in the same frequency as you; the town you were born in may not have the resources you're looking for. Some actions may not be in the same frequency as you; maybe drinking on the weekends is getting in the way of your goals.

The key word here is *filter*. Your brain will shoo away things you're not looking for and will realign to focus and recognize things you are looking for. Again, like attracts like. Your thoughts impact what you notice or pay attention to, so use this to your advantage.

Search for vibrational harmony while in pursuit of your vision. Align yourself with people, places, and things that will help you along your journey. But remember, it's about attracting, which requires focus. As noted, we can't simply wish for things to happen; it requires action—one of the essential steps in utilizing this law.

While focusing is an important aspect, we must ensure we are not overly focused. I know that may sound contradictory—explanation incoming.

We can't hyper-focus on the things we are looking to attract. If we do this, we will ironically realize that the results we're noticing oppose our original intention. But how can this be? This is known as the *backwards law*, as made famous by philosopher Alan Watts.

The backwards law is the idea that pursuing something, whether it is a feeling, a specific look, a physical object, a person, or whatever it may be, will only remind us we lack it. For example, constantly chasing happiness will only leave us with a feeling of dissatisfaction, as it reiterates that we lack it in the first place.[8]

"Wait a minute. Didn't you say the law of attraction is about focusing on our desire so we can attract said desire into our lives? But now you're saying if we focus on it too much, we'll get the opposite result. How does that make any sense?"

Whoa, slow down there.

The law of attraction concerns itself with attracting things by focusing on them—but we must not place too much emphasis on these things. There's a fine line—a happy medium, if you will. We don't want to worry or concern ourselves with these things too much. That will ultimately lead to obsession. This is not our goal, as too much concern for something could make you manic.

Here's a better way to look at it: The law of attraction concerns itself with *recognition*, which is strongly contrasted from obsession. Recognition is the other essential step for utilizing this law. Thankfully, I connected with an expert to discuss the law of attraction and how it connects to recognition.

Introducing Dr. D. Ivan Young, MCC, NBC-HWC, CPDC. One of the nation's most highly respected life coaches, he's also a TEDx speaker, behavioral modification and relationship expert, Presidential Lifetime Achievement Award recipient, Member of the Forbes Coaches Council, Fellow and Co-Lead for Race, Equity, and Inclusion at the Institute of Coaching McLean, and a Harvard Medical School affiliate.

Ladies and gentlemen, the accolades just keep coming.

Dr. Young is a law of attraction advocate who even has a viral TED Talk video where he presents this idea and discusses its importance. As I was researching for this book, this incredible human showed up on my radar.

Fast forward a little bit, and here we are, chatting with Dr. Young himself. Our conversation was phenomenal, his expertise unmatched. During our discussion, he graciously shared some of his wisdom so I may pass it on to others who are interested in learning about the law of attraction.

In our conversation, Dr. Young posed the question, "How are you using what's present and what is in your environment as a catalyst for your intention?"

This question gets to the core of recognition in the law of attraction. The universe will confirm that it hears you after you've declared what you want, but you must be able to recognize the signs it presents to you. Is there anything in your current environment that is a sign or indicator? Is there something that may be a portal or stepping stone for your desire?

This concept is similar to the classic car story you may hear when someone drives their new car. Perhaps you've acquired a new SUV, and now you've noticed SUVs all around town. It seems as if everyone suddenly has the same one as you do. Isn't that crazy? Well—not really.

It's not that everyone now has the same SUV. You're now noticing these vehicles passing by because they're on your mind due to your recent purchase. The law of attraction works in the same way. You're now recognizing more.

But wait, it gets deeper. Once we recognize it, we can let the universe take the wheel and show us things we couldn't even imagine were possible. We can do this by narrowing our expectations for our desires.

Now, what does this actually mean? It means we make our expectations bare bones, simplified. We do this by not becoming rigidly attached to one specific process, outcome, or desire. With this, we free ourselves from the frivolous stress that appears when we advance toward our goals as we let the universe handle the details.

Your vision should be specific in describing what it is you're looking for. Still, as mentioned, your vision should not be so overly attached to anything that may derive and be an outcome from it. Now, I'm not saying you should settle for less; quite the opposite, actually. If you recall, we are looking to lower our expectations, not our standards.

What I am saying is to be open-minded. While pursuing your newfound or preexisting goal or desire, do not neglect unfamiliar processes, outcomes, or potentially new desires. If you neglect such things, you will limit yourself.

When you become rigidly attached to a specific process, outcome, or desire, you are ridding yourself of all other possibilities that may serve you as well, if not more so. The universe may have a better idea about what you need than you do. You may discover what the universe offers you might be preferable compared to your initial want—open yourself to these possibilities.

Remember, we are ever-changing beings. Our goals and desires will likely change throughout our journey, or we may find something else that will serve us better. But, there's no way for this to happen if we are too attached to one possibility, as we may unknowingly block ourselves from other opportunities.

We must become open to all processes, outcomes, and potentially new desires to bring ourselves the best opportunities. This idea goes hand in hand with recognition. Be mindful, recognize the signs, and learn to identify *other* possibilities as well.

In all aspects, there may be another possibility that works for us we didn't even consider. We cannot be so attached to one specific idea about how our desire will come about that we neglect other potential possibilities. Do not limit yourself, be open to new opportunities, and see what the universe has in store for you.

LAW IN ACTION

Let's touch on an example that shows these steps in action. This will give you a better understanding of how the law of attraction works in a real-life scenario. The example includes all the primary steps you would apply while utilizing the law of attraction:

- Identify a goal.
- Narrow your expectations.
- Recognize the signs.
- Take action.

For instance, let's say you received news that you've got a child on the way. What a glorious day! While transitioning to become a more well-rounded and responsible adult for your child, you check on your financial status with your partner.

Oh no! It seems your finances aren't up to par with where they should be to be financially stable for this incoming child. Bummer. Time to level up.

What now? Well, it's time to attract money.

You've identified your goal, which is to make more money. Now, it's time to narrow your expectations—you put faith in yourself and the universe that somehow, through recognition and action, your goal will come to fruition. You make it clear that you are open to all processes and outcomes (and potentially new desires), as they will lead you to where you need to be. You trust the universe to make it happen.

From here, you then visualize ways to attract money. Perhaps you're thinking about ways to take advantage of your overtime hours, find a second job, sell things to make extra cash, etc. You even consider job hunting for something a little more lucrative.

While you're at work, you overhear someone chatting about Joe Schmo apparently transferring to a different department. It seems there's some movement in your organization. You hear another coworker mention they will open his position to internal candidates only.

Wow, there's an opportunity. That's something you weren't expecting— better, even. You've been waiting on a possible promotion into a similar position like Joe's for some time now. What are the chances?

Later, you notice that your CPR certification is almost expired. Oh no! It's crucial that you obtain this certification as it's required for your day-to-day tasks at work. You contact your supervisor and see what to do.

Your supervisor informs you that your organization will pay you to take another class over the weekend. You will need to put in some overtime hours on a Saturday, but you jump right on it. What an opportunity. It's just what you were looking for.

Later that day, you search the web for jobs. You are stunned by the number of openings nearby for your specific job. And guess what, they're all paying more than your current salary. But, wait. How can this be happening?

It's all happening because you're recognizing. You've identified a goal, which was to make more money, and now you're recognizing things in your immediate environment that could act as a catalyst for that goal.

Before identifying your goal, you would overlook things now drawing your attention, whether that's a promotion opportunity, an overtime opportunity, or anything that may help you out. These are not wild coincidences; you are now realizing opportunities as this new goal becomes imprinted in your mind's eye.

You see, you're not simply sitting on the floor wishing for things to happen; you are putting yourself in a position to attract money. There's no excessive hyper-focusing. You simply recognize opportunities when they arise. All that's left to do is to act.

Here's the bottom line. We can utilize the law of attraction by applying the primary steps: *identify your goal*, *narrow your expectation*, meaning open your mind to all possibilities, including new or different processes, outcomes, or desires; *recognize the signs* to discover what the universe can show you; and, most importantly, *take action*.

Now, why is the action part the most important? Well, the reason is twofold.

One, what would you get done if there was no action involved? Simple, nothing—nothing at all.

Two, action is more than simply seizing opportunities that arise from the law of attraction—it is about creating these opportunities too. In the next chapter, we'll discuss manifestation, which is the "planning and action" part of the law of attraction.

CHAPTER 4: MANIFESTATION

Manifestation means to take something theoretical and make it real. It is planning and taking action to turn our wants into reality.

To manifest, we must consider our desires and make a plan. We're looking to create said plan *before* we act so we do so properly and efficiently. Ultimately, this will help us clear our pathway to success and keep us on our path.

"Okay, so how does manifestation work?"

We can narrow down manifestation into *five basic steps*.

STEP 1: BE CLEAR ABOUT WHAT YOU WANT

First, create clear goals and desires. But fair warning, beware of creating goals and desires overly specific. While being specific when deciding what you want is fine, being overly specific may rigidly attach you to a particular process, outcome, or desire that will limit the other possibilities that the universe may have on offer.

Search for a happy medium. Define your goals in a clear way that isn't too vague, which will have you lost in the wind, or too overly specific, which will deny you satisfaction from any other possibilities that may serve you as well or better. Again, we want to lower our expectations, not our standards—so keep the goals you truly want, just don't become obsessed with the expectation of how you may obtain them.

Take some time to jot these down. Be clear and visualize them often. Talk to others about what it is you want and put it out in the universe.

STEP 2: SHED LIMITING BELIEFS

Your current beliefs are the determining factors for what you allow yourself to achieve. Your beliefs alter everything; they change your world and how you maneuver through life. You must make sure you create and maintain a strong self-belief that will help you move toward your vision.

If you're feeling blocked or limited, you may need to reevaluate. Consider your beliefs and their authenticity. I recommend taking some time to see where you feel limited. Question the origin of these beliefs. Where did they come from? Formulate questions that will help you understand the root cause of your limiting beliefs. Search for facts and debunk these narratives that hold you back.

STEP 3: PLAN AND EXECUTE

After you write down your clearly defined goals or desires, you can develop your execution plan. This step is to hold you accountable—there are no if, ands, or buts. If you want something, you have to go for it.

No one will knock on your door one day and say, "Hey! Here's that opportunity you've wanted so bad but never did anything about!" Don't shoot the messenger, but that's never going to happen. If you want something, you must get off your ass and get it.

Put in the time, conduct research, contact others, and create your plan. Put yourself in a position to learn more about what it takes to reach your goals. Once you've collected enough information, TAKE ACTION.

Create a custom plan that is specific and consistent. For example, if you want to manifest better grades in school, create a schedule of times loaded with activities that will help you achieve just that. Keep this goal or desire in your mind's eye and be on the lookout for opportunities in your environment that may assist you in reaching this goal or desire.

STEP 4: PRACTICE GRATITUDE

Progress is progress, no matter how big or small. When you're manifesting, it's crucial to stay consistent. Again, when we want something, this isn't as difficult; but it's ridiculous not to expect any difficulties along the way.

You may go through the wringer at times, but you must persevere. Brace that storm, learn from your mistakes and challenging times, and come out stronger. Meanwhile, when we are fortunate enough to catch these glimpses of success along the way (again, no matter how big or small), it's crucial we take the time to give thanks.

Keep a journal and write down everything going well. Celebrate opportunities and small wins and identify the new lessons you've learned from losses. Also, take time to write down things that aren't going so well, alongside ways to fix these issues for next time. And, periodically, look back to see how far you've come in your process. But don't look back for too long; you're not going that way.

STEP 5: TRUST THE PROCESS

Letting go and trusting the process is often the most challenging step. Remember, good things take time, and this stuff isn't easy. If it was, you would've done it already. So, stay clear on your path and keep moving forward.

Fell down? Get up! Dust your clothes off and move along. If you want it, let nothing get in your way. There is no instant gratification or shortcuts here. While going through this process, trust it. Put your head down and do the work. And when you look up, things might look a whole lot different.

If you rush the process, you're detracting from the flow of it all. The universe knows when the time is right. Forcing something may take away from the process, which may hold critical lessons, or a potentially better outcome, which you may miss.

Don't stress the timing of reaching your vision. Sure, having a timeframe will help get you going and work more consistently, which is helpful in the long run, but we don't want to fool ourselves. When it's time, it's time.

The universe will do whatever it needs to do. Trust in the natural unfolding of events and do your best to feel good along the way.

Be patient with yourself. All good things take time. Keep your goals in mind and remind yourself what you are working for. If it's not worth waiting the extra time to receive, is it truly something that you want?

CHAPTER 5: INTUITION

A group of researchers at Michigan State University have made an extraordinary discovery. They've concluded that our stomachs contain specific components of our nervous system and that humans have—what they call—a "second brain." At some point, you've had a "gut feeling" about something. That gut feeling is your second brain at work.

This secondary brain—also known as our enteric nervous system (ENS)— is a collection of brain-like neurons and neurotransmitters that reside in our stomach and can influence many things, including our judgment.

The second brain is not the root of real thoughts or decisions but informs our state of mind in more obscure ways. For example, when we feel butterflies in our stomach, that's a signal from the gut, warning us of a physiological stress response.[1]

ENS specialist at the University of California, Los Angeles, and author of *The Mind-Gut Connection*, Dr. Emeran Mayer, states that our ENS comprises 50 to 100 million nerve cells. That's the same number of nerve cells that reside in our spinal cord. Mayer says that our gut has capabilities that surpass all of our other organs and potentially even rival our brain.[2]

The vagus nerve carries a wide range of signals from our digestive system and other organs to the brain and vice versa. Around 80% of the vagus nerve devotes its time to reporting information to the brain. When these signals flow back and forth, they can influence our mood, decision-making, and overall well-being. It would appear evident, thanks to the vagus nerve, that having a "gut feeling" is quite a real thing.[3]

"This is cool and all, but what does this have to do with my vision?"

Good question. The answer is this: with our vision, it's apparent that things will try to get in our way. Negative thoughts, doubt, and worry play lead roles in preventing us from making the uncomfortable jump to our new happy place—we can attribute this to fear.

You see, fear is what we believe to be rational. The key word here is *believe*. Fear is not always correct. We don't know everything. Consider that there are ideas, theories, perspectives, and other similar things invisible to us.

When we taint ourselves with pessimistic assumptions, ideas, perspectives, and beliefs, we restrict ourselves. Ultimately, this leads to ridiculous thought processes that tell us we cannot achieve something. Remember that these negative assumptions are complete bullshit.

While fear creates the belief we are "rationalizing," our intuition provides room for instinct, which ultimately brings us into action. Our intuition is our ability to understand something without the need for conscious reasoning. More simply, intuition concerns itself with less thought and more action.

Far too often in life, by the time we realize we are overthinking, it's too late. This is a war between intellect and instinct. Intuition allows us to act without processing everything that's happening; it's simply our reaction. Fear can alter this, especially in our life decisions and perspectives as sometimes it provides for too much "rational" thinking.

David Vobora, former linebacker for the Los Angeles Rams and the Seattle Seahawks, gave a TED Talk on intuition and the "second brain" at Southern Methodist University in Dallas.

After some context about his experience with the fight between intellect and instinct, he explained that fear locks us into conformity. He adds that fear can make us buy into others' expectations of what our lives should look like, which will rob us of our true inclinations.[4]

With your vision, you must not let fear get in your way. Being intuitive while pursuing a sincere desire is essential to our success. It would help if you stopped thinking so much. If it feels right, go for it. By all means necessary, do not let fear get in the way.

Fear is usually false. Most of the time, these fearful thoughts are just that— thoughts. Don't get it twisted; most of the time, our fear may come to light as false, but being near danger is real. Feeling fear in the face of danger is a good thing, but it may be essential to consider facing this fear when it's over something that you or someone else may conclude as silly.

"How can we deal with fear while we build our vision?"

There are two tactics for dealing with fear: *following your intuition* and *detachment* (we'll get to this one).

"But how can we possibly stay on our path if our 'rationalized' fear can effortlessly push us off track?"

This is where manifestation comes into play—*you must stick with your plan*. Make sure you've developed your plan with careful consideration. Make this plan concrete. It should be solid enough that you can refer to it and find comfort in its reliability and precision.

Also, feeling fear is normal, especially when trekking in new territory. But keep going; follow your plan and your intuition until you've obtained your goal or desire.

Throughout your journey, hold yourself accountable and stay on your path, regardless of others, who will inevitably try to intervene. It's up to you to make it happen. Remember, everyone's entitled to their own opinion, and that's fine. The problem begins when you let others' opinions affect you.

Evaluate reason, but on your own terms. And don't believe those who tell you otherwise. They're not more "realistic"; they're assholes whose vision is strictly designed to see only on the surface level. Do your thing; trust yourself.

"What if it doesn't work out at first? What if I feel discouraged?"

Keep going. Change and growth are not linear. Change is a roller coaster and growth does not come easy. After time has passed, you may look back briefly and realize the progress you've made. Remember, perfection doesn't exist. We're bound to have bumps in the road, so aim for progress, not perfection.

Now, before we get too far off track, let's get back to the science lesson.

By actively tending to our mental health through positive practice, we can reduce our anxiety and worry. In recent years, it's becoming clear that the ENS influences our brain at deeper levels than we had initially thought. Evidence is emerging that the ENS affects our mood and even plays a role in depression.

Dr. Vincent Candrawinata, a researcher at the University of Newcastle, expands on the influence of our ENS. He states this nervous system actually operates independently of our brain and that it controls our entire digestive system and body system, including our mental state.

Dr. Candrawinata posits that neurological issues and digestive health are linked, and studies have shown a connection between mental health issues and low levels of healthy bacteria in our gut. Dr. Candrawinata cautions we must take good care of ourselves and our gut and suggests we take action with proper diets, sleep, exercise, and supporting supplements.[5]

Ah, yes. We did it. Science lesson adjourned. So, what was the reason for all this information? Well, it's simple. Your intuition enables a feeling of *knowing* without conscious reasoning. Overanalyzing things such as your vision or your goals will ultimately lead to a "convincing" story that will keep you from reaching these things.

Therefore, follow your intuition. The science is there, folks. The proof is in the pudding.

We can't rationalize everything. As human beings, we aren't that intelligent yet. In our history, we've done pretty unbelievable things, been to space, cloned a sheep, invented airplanes, built the pyramids, and the list goes on and on.

But we've not yet been able to solve every single thing. And honestly, we never will. There are just certain things we will never have the answers to. But, you know what? That's okay. We have our intuition.

Life is full of uncertainty. Take note of this. We can't plan everything. If we attempt to plan everything, it can go one of two ways: everything will go your way, and you will have no room for growth or any new and exciting experiences, or nothing will go your way, and you will feel distraught. Remember this while you continue on your journey toward your goals and desires.

So, in times of uncertainty, trust your intuition. Most importantly and above all—*trust yourself.*

CHAPTER 6: DETACHMENT

Let's revisit this idea of fear.

While intuition may assist us in certain aspects of our (at times) fear-filled minds, detachment may bring another bit of relief when we're overwhelmed with feelings or fears we can't seem to let go of.

Jay Shetty is a life coach, former monk, and author of the masterpiece, *Think Like a Monk*, where he explores fear and detachment through the lens of the wisdom he obtained through his time as a monk. From ancient monk teachings, we learn we must improve our skills and self-control so we may not become bothered by external stimuli, such as the opinions of others and things happening outside our control.

According to Shetty, the cause of fear is our fixation on attachment. With that said, a primary cure for fear is *detachment*. We are constantly holding on to the things we believe we own. Whether it's a physical object, person, or something we identify with, we are always trying to hold on to or control these things. Although, everything is borrowed. So, when we hang on to these things, it gives them power over us.[1]

The Bhagavad Gita is a Hindu holy scripture that nails the ideologies behind detachment. The Bhagavad Gita teaches us that "detachment means you own nothing and nothing owns you."[2] Usually, detachment is thought to be pushing something away or, more often, disconnecting from it completely.

This perspective from the Bhagavad Gita inverts our common perception of detachment. Detachment is pursuing our lives the way we wish without feeling like we are consumed by it. For example, we often identify with emotions that are not ours to identify with. Emotions come and go—they are not ours to keep.

But, because we identify with emotions so much, we believe that we *are* these emotions. Detachment teaches us that these emotions are not ours; they are loaned to us. You are not sad—you are feeling sad. You are not happy—you are feeling happy.

We do not have default emotions, although believing we do will undoubtedly keep these feelings around. When these emotions arise, note them as mere experiences.

We are not these emotions, and these emotions are not us. Don't fall for it. Our emotions, like our thoughts, come and go. They are just temporary experiences.

We must not identify with them because they are not permanent. They are simply part of the human experience. Once we understand this, the thoughts and emotions we experience tend not to bother us because we know that they will soon pass and that life goes on.

Sally Kempton, an author, former monk, and internationally recognized teacher of meditation and yoga philosophy, was generous enough to share her take on detachment with me. Throughout our conversation, Kempton shared her infinite wisdom on detachment, alongside some compelling ideologies.

According to Kempton, there are two types of detachment: genuine detachment and false detachment.

Genuine detachment starts with recognizing your own reactions, emotions, and *stories* about an event, allowing yourself to feel these things, and accepting the fact that you are in a state of attachment. This includes (most of the time) accepting the discomfort of not getting what you want. From here, you can practice accepting the reality of the situation—the loss or unwanted event—letting go of the reaction and then consciously letting go of the desire or clinging that is causing the overbearing feeling that comes along with attachment. It's important to note that this may take a few attempts before it clicks as detachment has to do with having a high-degree of acceptance—which certainly doesn't come easy. Genuine detachment is not possible unless you are first willing to feel the discomfort or loss of not getting what you want.

Genuine detachment derives from experience, generally through many years of life, or by learning from repetitive situations. When faced with something difficult, you understand that *this too shall pass*; from there, you're able to detach from living with attachment, which can cause pain and fear. It's about having an authentic internal agreement and understanding that everything is temporary—thoughts and emotions included—which will allow you to let go and move forward without getting stuck or feeling overly attached to a particular thing.

False detachment usually arises from the desire to bypass any feelings of discomfort or hurt by prematurely telling yourself "I'm fine" or "I don't really care" rather than facing the attachment, feeling it, and going through the process of letting go.

This detachment is often associated with disassociation—an idea that implies that individuals without the proper internal agreement and understanding of genuine detachment will pursue false detachment and disassociate themselves from things like their relationships, ambitions, and possessions.

Detachment doesn't mean being distant from everything; it's about being close to everything and not allowing it to control you. It's about learning how to navigate these situations in life. We can't avoid things like our relationships, ambitions, and possessions, as they are a crucial part of life itself.[3]

Eventually, disassociating ourselves from these things may deprive us of our inner lives. In one of Kempton's blogs, she notes that "engagement with people and places, skills and ideas, money and possessions is what grounds inner practice in reality."[4] To her, the pressure from external relationships will make it easier to learn compassion, reason through anger, and take action.

Detachment is not about external things but internal acceptance derived from experience. Genuine detachment is acquired through many years of life or specific experiences. It's seeing how different modes of behavior create anxiety and pain and then learning how to disentangle cords and habits that cause the anxiety and pain.

Even simpler, it's an understanding that life goes on and that we should go with it.

If we're attached, we can get hurt, plain and simple. When we become attached, we open ourselves up to a potential blow without even noticing it. Recognize the attachments in your life.

"Wait a second. If we constantly acknowledge all of the impermanence in our lives, how can we truly enjoy it? If we own nothing, what is ours? Is anything ours?"

Easy there. Don't worry. Detachment sounds like an overwhelming concept, but we'll cover these questions.

First off, we should note that everything is borrowed.

"Everything?"

Yes, everything. Your job, your car, your house, your family, your friends, your feelings, your thoughts, your life—*everything*. These things are not ours to keep but ours to borrow, use, and enjoy for a period.

When attached to anything borrowed, whatever it is can have power over us. These attachments can cause us pain and distribute fear into our lives. This is a widespread concern, but we're all borrowers. You, me, and even those with perfect lives on Instagram. Yes—even Kanye West is a borrower.

We're all humans going through this similar, bizarre experience. It's ineffable as it touches both sides of the spectrum. Life is incredible and overwhelming. But that's the human experience.

There's always good and bad. It's yin and yang, or light and dark.

"So, how do we stop these things from having power over us?"

We can see the bigger picture when we accept that everything around us is borrowed. When we realize everything is lent to us, we can replace our worry and fear about losing these things with a feeling of freedom and gratitude for having them in the first place. Detachment can bring us freedom and gratitude, but it's a game of perspective.

For instance, do you know what the odds are of you actually existing? You've probably heard an array of answers. Most likely, you may have heard that it is one in 400 trillion. Now, while these odds are jaw-dropping themselves, others would argue they are false.

Dr. Ali Binazir, a happiness engineer, executive speaking consultant, and author, begs to differ. After reading this estimation, Dr. Binazir crunched his own numbers.

There were many excruciating calculations, including a long list of factors to consider such as the probability of our parent's meeting, the likelihood of the right sperm meeting the right egg, etc. After all this, he kindly placed the calculations onto an aesthetically pleasing infographic.

Long story short, the probability of you existing at all is 1 in $10^{2,685,000}$.[5] Yes, that's a 10 with over 2.5 million zeros after it.

"What exactly does that mean?"

According to Dr. Binazir, it's the probability of two million people coming together to play dice, and the dice they roll will collectively have a trillion sides. Let's say each person—of two million—rolls their dice, and they all, miraculously, land on the same number.[6] That, my friend, is the probability of you existing.

It goes a little further than one in 400 trillion, huh? Let that soak in.

Okay, so what am I getting at? We're on the profit side. We came from nothing, with zero investments, and we left an unbelievable number of potential humans behind. We are the chosen ones. We made it. This is our time, and we cannot waste it.

50

Now, let's tie this example into detachment. Detachment can bring freedom and gratitude, but it's all about perspective. If we're looking at life as something that is "ours," then we're in for a rude awakening. And if we're living in constant fear that something that we believe is ours may be taken away, it can cause anxiety.

But, here's the kicker. If we realize that everything is borrowed, we can bring forth more gratitude and a different, more appreciative outlook on life. When you're on vacation, you don't spend every minute worrying about it being over, do you? No! Of course not.

Instead, you understand that your vacation won't last forever; thus, you enjoy it more. You know that it's something you won't always be able to do. This approach can work the same in life.

If we utilize the principles of detachment in our lives, we can reduce our amount of fear. When we can identify these fears, we can change our perspectives and relationships with them through detachment. This concept works in all aspects of life, on both a large and small scale.

We've become attached to things, people, and outcomes beyond our control. This sparks fear in our lives. But, with a high degree of acceptance, we learn how to come to terms with how we don't own or control anything. Furthermore, we can stop letting these external things control us.

The bottom line is this: We can't control everything. But we can control our reactions. Internally, we make our own choices and control things within ourselves. And come to discover —that's all we ever need.

CHAPTER 7: AUTOSUGGESTION & AFFIRMATIONS

It's the late 1800s in Troyes, a beautiful town in northeastern France filled with Gothic churches that have jolting stained glass windows. In Troyes lives an apothecary (pharmacist) by the name of Émile Coué.[1]

Émile wasn't just any regular apothecary; he was known as a man of the people. He genuinely cared for his patients—consistently reassuring his clients by raving about each remedy's efficiency and significance. After some time, Coué discovered something incredible from his patients, which later came to be known as the placebo effect.[2]

Coué later realized that his patients had complete faith in him. They undoubtedly stood behind his medical practices and beliefs and had the utmost confidence that the prescribed medicine would work. With curiosity, he took a closer look at this situation.

Impressed by the results of his patients, Coué studied hypnosis. Eventually, he narrowed his attention to a form of self-hypnosis he called autosuggestion.[3]

"What is autosuggestion?"

It's the hypnotic or subconscious adoption of an idea someone has to create from within themselves. It is a form of self-induced suggestion where individuals will ultimately guide their own thoughts, feelings, or behaviors. Coué believed this is what his patients were accomplishing. It was evident through his observations that his patients would receive better and faster results with a firm belief in his medical practices.[4]

He then created the Coué method and published his first book, *Self Mastery Through Conscious Autosuggestion*. The book was published in 1920 in England and published again later in the United States.

The Coué method is a routine of verbal repetition, a mantra or phrase we can repeatedly use throughout our day. Coué believed we could change our perspectives and urges by changing our subconscious thoughts and behaviors. He believed this could only happen by using our imagination.[5] Essentially, it's using our conscious mind to repeat ideas and phrases, thus influencing our subconscious mind over time.

When our will and imagination are antagonistic, the imagination will win without exception.[6] Coué's research supports this statement, as he defines autosuggestion as "the influence of the imagination upon the moral and physical being of mankind."[7]

Our imaginations are powerful. Coué suggests that our minds are powerful enough to alter our subconscious minds, thus molding our thoughts, feelings, and behaviors into precisely how we consciously choose them to be.

Sure, there were skeptics. But he was right. If you recall from earlier in this book, when we were learning about the law of attraction, with consistency and mental conditioning, the quality of thoughts in our conscious mind can heavily influence the state of our subconscious mind.

Current data confirms this idea. Our bodies are physically changing in response to our thoughts. Remember, our subconscious thoughts affect our vibrational frequency. When we think, our brain releases neurotransmitters; these chemicals control our body's functions.[8]

Now, it's important to note we can utilize this idea for our own benefit.

"How exactly do we do that?"

Cue *affirmations*! Using affirmations, which are mantras or phrases that bring emotional support and encouragement, is a primary technique we can use to practice autosuggestion. It's a practical way to apply self-induced suggestions and begin to consciously change our subconscious minds, which will alter our vibrational frequency.

One study used functional magnetic resonance imaging (fMRI) to show that affirmations can activate the brain's reward system. The researchers also found increased activity in key regions of the brain's self-processing and valuation systems.[9]

Our brain is powerful, more so than we may recognize. Coué believed that our own beliefs determined the degree of this power. In his book, *Self Mastery Through Conscious Autosuggestion*, Coué states that if you convince yourself that you can do something, provided it's possible, you can do it. But, if you convince yourself you cannot do something, no matter how simple, it will be impossible to complete.[10]

Coué's evidence would suggest that when we believe we can achieve something, there's no stopping us. He emphasized believing in ourselves and stated that in the battle of will versus imagination, the imagination will *always* win.[11]

Coué used the example of walking across a wooden plank to illustrate this idea. Let's say we have a wooden plank: it's 30 feet long by 1 foot wide, and we placed it down across the floor.

We probably could walk across it with ease, keeping ourselves balanced and avoiding the floor beneath it. Coué argues that the reason we're able to do this is that we believe we can.

Don't believe me? Okay, here's Coué's counterpoint example: Let's say this plank connected two high points of a cathedral with a death-defying drop beneath.

Now, walking across this seems like no easy job, right? But what's the difference? Regardless of the consequence, it's the same task (assuming we exclude other factors like wind and such). So, why does one seem much more doable than the other? It's because we *believe* we're able to do so.[12]

After some experiments, Coué discovered that subjects could not be hypnotized against their will. They must take belief into their own hands and genuinely provide some trust in these processes and themselves.

Coué notes this and suggests that if a doctor prescribes medication to a patient with no comment, the remedies provided won't succeed as well as they could. But if the doctor provides positive reinforcement, it will produce specific and better results; he states these results are practically certain.[13]

"Okay, okay. But, how does this help?"

Well, this provides evidence that autosuggestion and affirmations work. They always have. We can use autosuggestion to add positivity to our lives. As mentioned, a key way to practice autosuggestion is by creating and utilizing affirmations.

Coué had a famous and universal affirmation he would suggest his patients use: "Every day, in every respect, I am getting better and better." He would tell his patients to emphasize these words as they apply to every mental and physical need. He used to recommend we say these out loud 20 times in the morning and before bed.[14]

So, what can you take away from this chapter? First, believe in yourself. Sometimes, it's up to you to be your biggest fan. Second, remember that we can influence the subconscious mind to accept whatever idea or thought we choose by repeatedly adding those ideas and thoughts to our conscious mind.[15]

With that, create an affirmation that suits you best and stay committed. With some repetition and time, you will see results. Remember, our imagination is powerful—it's time we use it.

PART II — WELLNESS

What is wellness? Wellness is the daily act of practicing healthy habits to obtain better physical and mental health outcomes. It's the constant pursuit of a more optimal, healthy, and fulfilling life.

More often than not, people will agree that wellness has many facets. In this book, we've broken wellness into four dimensions: spiritual, physical, emotional, and social.

If you're wondering why wellness is a part of this book and what it has to do with your vision, the answer is simple: wellness, in any aspect, can improve your overall quality of life.

Enhancing all avenues of wellness will help you take care of your body and mind, which makes it easier to take strides toward an optimal life. Forget the standard baseline for wellness. We're searching for more.

We're looking to thrive in all avenues of wellness; we're looking to live a more fulfilled life, live a healthier lifestyle, manage our stress more efficiently, and connect more often with those around us. These are things we can experience on a deeper and more meaningful level when we immerse ourselves in life and tend to all the dimensions of wellness more often.

As we explore wellness, consider your vision. Think more about how you're feeling, how you're thinking, how things around you are looking. As we continue, examine which areas of wellness may need some improvement. There will be something from each dimension of wellness you can apply to your life.

DIMENSION 1: SPIRITUAL WELLNESS

Spirituality is a major component of wellness. But what is spirituality, and what does this have to do with wellness? Spirituality is a broad concept defined in many ways.

Essentially, it is a sense of something bigger than us; usually, it involves searching for meaning in life. This search is often an incredible experience that provides us with a deep sense of being alive.

"Okay, but how does this tie into wellness?"

Well, using plenty of introspection, we're able to articulate what *our* lives are all about and come to understand more clearly what we value.

Spiritual wellness involves finding your own meaning or purpose, thus finding a greater sense of self. It refers to our morals, values, and beliefs; when appropriately utilized (according to us), our more straightforward path tells us where to go. We take these core beliefs that we've created and allow them to guide us through life.

Spirituality is about experiencing life according to *your* life's purpose and moral values. It's about connecting with ourselves and making sure we're taking the right path—or, rather, the path right for *us*. When we connect with ourselves, we open doors to a more meaningful and optimal life.

When we've identified this path, we can use it as a sense of direction. It stops us from frantically moving through life without a trajectory or vision. It all ties back to our vision.

We can practice spiritual wellness in various ways. This includes practicing *meditation* and *gratitude*. Believe it or not, spiritual wellness practices have incredible health benefits such as reduced stress, lower levels of depression and anxiety, and positive mood boosts. These practices can also help us develop our *spiritual strength*.

"What in the world is spiritual strength?"

It's a driving force, the fuel that drives our ambition and can give us motivation. It's why we get up in the morning and what helps us decide for the greater good.

Spiritual strength can derive from various influences: experiences, role models, family, friends, and other types of inspirations. When our spiritual strength is in good condition, then we're in good condition.

But now, let's jump into the next chapter and discuss a key tactic in practicing spiritual wellness known as *meditation*.

CHAPTER 8: MEDITATION

Your mind is like the sky. When you're feeling like yourself and things are aligned, the sky is wide open and as blue as you can imagine. Here, everything is good; you're feeling strong and the mind is clear. But by nature, we can expect visitors—in this case, clouds. These clouds represent our thoughts and emotions. Every so often (or sometimes, too often), clouds arrive and block our view of the beautiful blue sky, which is our true self.

At times, too many clouds may emerge and block the blue sky. After some time with this cloud cover, we may forget about the blue sky. We may feel down as we notice the storm clouds rolling in, bound to come with heavy thunder and lightning. And because we've forgotten about the blue sky, we're feeling lost and scared, with nowhere to turn.

Sound familiar? Well, if you consider yourself an overthinker, worrier, or anything of the sort, you may know this all too well. This is a metaphor for overthinking, something that grabs us and slams us down occasionally. It's difficult to break free from this cycle of getting caught up in our head. But fear not: there's a tactic known as meditation that may help with such an issue.

Meditation can help us separate ourselves from the clouds. It can help us remember that the blue sky is always present, even when we can't see it. Thoughts or emotions (or in this instance, clouds) are free flowing. They come and go, backwards and forwards, all day long. And when we become too concerned with these thoughts or emotions, they can consume us.

They can be so overwhelming that we forget what they are: just thoughts and emotions, nothing more. It's vital to remember that the blue sky, or our true self, is always there, no matter how much cloud coverage there is.

We don't have to identify with these thoughts or emotions. Thoughts and emotions come and go. They are a piece of the whole pie known as the human experience. Knowing that alone will bring us peace.

Understanding this concept will give us permission to kick back and simply watch the clouds pass by, as we know the blue sky is sitting right behind them. We know our true beliefs, and these unwanted thoughts and emotions cannot tell us otherwise. *We are not these thoughts* as they are not us, and *we are not these emotions* as they are not us.

"Okay, but how does this all tie into meditation?"

The brain is like a muscle: use it or lose it. We train our brains similarly to how we may train our pets. If we do something repeatedly, that thing eventually becomes a habit. And utilizing meditation is one way we can train our brains. If we can train our brains to identify and recognize the particular behaviors holding us back, we can let these behaviors go and stop them from bothering us.

Essentially, with meditation, we are looking to give ourselves space between the *real* us and the thoughts and emotions that race through our minds and bodies. Thankfully, meditation gives us a space to consciously differentiate between these things so we may see with more clarity and act accordingly.

"Interesting. Tell me more."

In 2011, a group of Harvard-affiliated researchers at Massachusetts

General Hospital (MGH) conducted a study on mindful meditation. In this study, magnetic resonance (MR) images were taken of the brain structure of 16 participants. The MR images were taken two weeks before and after undergoing the eight-week Mindfulness-Based Stress Reduction Program, which took place at the University of Massachusetts Center for Mindfulness. A control group (who did not practice meditation throughout the study) was used to compare and contrast results.[1]

Each of the 16 participants had been asked to keep track of how often they practiced mindful meditation each day. MR images were also taken of the non-meditators group throughout a similar timeframe. The group who meditated frequently reported spending an average of 27 minutes each day practicing these mindfulness exercises.[2]

Before the study began, each participant completed a mindfulness questionnaire; when they filled it out post-study, the results showed signs of significant improvement compared to the first questionnaire.[3]

After careful examination of the participants' brains, the researchers found increased gray-matter density in the hippocampus, known for learning and memory, and in structures associated with self-awareness, compassion, and introspection.[4]

There was also decreased gray-matter density in the amygdala, which plays a vital role in anxiety and stress. This discovery aligned with the participants' self-reports of decreased stress levels. No changes were found in the control group.[5]

Britta Hölzel, a Research Fellow at MGH and Giessen University in Germany, explores the subject of meditation in her research, explaining that we can actively change our brain structure and enhance our wellness to improve our quality of life with our meditation practice.[6]

Now, isn't that incredible? Research shows us that meditation can produce measurable changes in our brains. It can *literally* change our brain structure. Consider the changes in the brain that resulted from an eight-week program. Now consider how much we could change the brain for the better if we dedicated a significant portion of time to meditation alongside other helpful tactics.

Remember, however, that meditation is not a magic idea that will make all of your problems disappear; rather, it is a mindfulness tool. Mindfulness is the state of being aware, and when we utilize mindfulness tools, we dedicate time to introspection while reaping these great health benefits.

Meditation comes with the opportunity to exercise new perspectives, ideas, and concepts. It gives us a space to deal with these things. When in a state of serenity via meditation, we can look at aspects of our life from alternative angles and find new and unique ways to solve our problems. We can find clarity and finally stop letting our minds rule us—whether with negativity, worry, overthinking, or whatever is bothering you.

"But wait. Why would our own minds do such a thing, like try to rule us? Why do we even think negative thoughts in the first place?"

It's clear that none of us want these thoughts, so why do we have them? This reaches way back, long before us. In early human history, it was crucial to consider the negative scenarios that may happen, as this was a matter of life or death. Back then, it was a little more severe than it is today, considering the excess danger lurking around every corner.

"So, why are we still worried about negative things today?"

Well, the straightforward answer is that our brains are wired this way. We're hardwired for negativity. This tendency to think with negative thoughts is a tactic our brain utilizes to keep us safe. It's a defense mechanism.

This is the limbic system or the "threat system" of your brain at work. While it can aggravate, humans would probably not have survived without a properly functioning limbic system.[7]

Our limbic system's job is to keep us safe by evaluating whether something is considered a threat. If our limbic system perceives something as a threat, it will send a wave of neurophysiological activity to fulfill one goal: keep us safe. When this response is suitable, it is helpful. But sometimes this response may be unsuitable and may just get in our way (e.g., worrying when it's unnecessary).

If we have a skewed perspective or an issue that remains unaddressed, we could unknowingly create scenarios for our threat system to act when action is unnecessary. If we continue to let our limbic system have too much control over us, we may act unsuitably, which ultimately will inconvenience us as it is unnecessary.[8]

"What does this have to do with meditation?"

As mentioned, this is one reason we're practicing meditation: *we're giving ourselves space between the real us and the thoughts and emotions that arise.* We're becoming more mindful. We're putting ourselves in a clearer state of mind and shifting our awareness. This is a skill that can help us in all areas of life.

Emotions come and go and are not ours to identify with. When we purposely place ourselves in an area of calm and clarity, we can better evaluate the situations we're in and the experiences we're having. This will help us accept these emotions without identifying with them, further allowing them not to bother us.

"But why would I accept these emotions if they're unwanted?"

When you accept emotions, it doesn't mean these emotions are suddenly *wanted*. No one wants to feel anxious, worried, or fearful. But when we accept our emotions, it means we understand where they're coming from; it's an understanding of what these emotions actually are. They are not our true beliefs—*they are not authentic or true.*

The same is true of our thoughts. When we accept them, it's not because we believe them. It's because we understand where they're coming from, and they are *not true*. This way, we can better allow for thoughts and emotions to flow in and out without becoming attached to them or identifying with them.

When we understand this, these emotions tend not to bother us as we now know what they are—just emotions. Typically, we only have a problem with emotions when we feel like they're not supposed to be there. When this happens, we create resistance to said emotions.

Meditation creates space for us to consciously consider the thoughts and emotions that bother us; here, we can accurately gauge their authenticity. Meditation teaches us to observe, accept, and let go of thoughts and emotions instead of resisting them. These annoying feelings that emerge are temporary; note their ephemeral nature so you may not take them as seriously. I find it's important to note that we can *feel and not follow* our emotions and *think and not follow* our thoughts.

When you feel an emotion, acknowledge it, as strong or as subtle as it may be, and then come back to the present. Remind yourself that all emotions are a part of the human experience and understand these emotions have come to pass, as our thoughts do. We are not them and they are not us. We do not have to follow said emotions. Learning to accept these emotions will set us free; only then can we learn to not be a slave to our own minds.

When thoughts arise that are inaccurate or inauthentic, tend to them in the same way as your emotions. Acknowledge them, note them as just thoughts, and come back to the present. Occasionally, our minds overflow with thoughts, and they can be overwhelming. Gauging the authenticity of these thoughts can help us see them for what they are: nonsense. This will help us release them and move forward instead of resisting them. After some time, you'll find these random thoughts are not worth entertaining in the first place.

Resisting our thoughts and emotions is a dangerous game. If we continue doing so, eventually, we'll be tending to every thought and emotion that comes our way to justify, solve, or trace it, thus leading to an endless feedback loop of wondering and worrying about why we think or feel a particular way. Try not to suppress these emotions, as that only brings them on stronger.

It is possible to carry on with our lives without the baggage that these thoughts and emotions provide. Believe it or not, we have the option to leave them at the door. Here's where meditation comes into play.

If we implement a meditation practice into our lives, we can give ourselves a practical opportunity to consciously differentiate our true beliefs, thoughts, and emotions with a calm state of mind. The more we practice, the more skillful we'll become.

We should treat the brain as a muscle: either use it or lose it. Once we become more skilled in recognizing the differences between our true beliefs and random thoughts and emotions, we can more easily diffuse stressful situations that said thoughts and emotions create. We can let them go.

When we bring ourselves into a calm state, we can observe our thoughts and emotions with no judgment. We can note each thought or emotion that arises in the mind or the body. From there, we can lightly and easily return to our meditation practice without drifting too far into thought.

This experience can show us we need not follow these thoughts or emotions, thus detaching ourselves from these things. This will allow us to trust in our true beliefs and not be as bothered by the random thoughts and emotions we all receive.

Besides this, we can also use meditation to practice stillness, relax, and be more present—which are useful when building your optimal life.

Now, let's turn to a basic meditation walkthrough that you can try on your own. This one gives you the feel of a *basic* meditation session, but there are many different meditation practices for you to try.

Search the web for new meditation practices that may serve you better on any day. There are guided meditation videos all over the web. Different types of guided meditation practices include meditation for detachment, for being more present, for worry, acceptance, appreciation, and the list goes on. Each specific type of meditation practice has a question or prompt to guide you to better tend to the particular issue you are exploring or working on. Try out different meditation practices and see which types work best for you.

So, without further ado, let's give this a try.

MEDITATION WALKTHROUGH

FIND A QUIET LOCATION: Find a quiet place to sit, somewhere you know you won't be bothered. Sometimes, time is of the essence. Consider waking up earlier to find a tranquil atmosphere. As far as seating, some people prefer the floor, although finding a comfy chair with a pillow for back support doesn't hurt either. Whatever is the most comfortable.

DEEP BREATHING: With your eyes open, take a few deep breaths. In through the nose, hold for a few seconds, and exhale out through the mouth. Wait a few seconds, then do that again. Gazing softly ahead, repeat this three to four times. On the final deep breath, gently close your eyes.

FEEL YOUR BREATH: Let the breath return to its normal rhythm. Don't worry if you find this difficult; it's normal to feel like you must control your breath. Try not to let the mind control the breath; let the mind follow the breath.

Pretend there's a camera in front of you, and you're watching yourself through that camera. You're not controlling anything. You're simply watching yourself breathe without force, inhaling and exhaling naturally. Focus on this for a minute if you can.

NOTICE YOUR BODY: Scan your body from top to bottom. Start with your head and neck area. Assess the current state of that area. Do your best to notice how that area of your body feels. From there, relax that particular area.

Continue with this: check your shoulder area, torso, thighs, and calves. Keep scanning your body, down to your toes. The point is to maintain focus and unlock relaxation in areas of your body that may unknowingly hold tension.

NOTICE MIND-WANDERING: Please note that your mind will wander. This is normal. The idea is to notice that your mind has wandered, then gently return to your breath. Make it effortless.

Remember, meditation need not be perfect. It's about mindfulness; we want to simply notice what our mind is doing. If your mind drifts frequently, don't fret; you'll improve at this with practice. Permit yourself to let go of whatever your mind drifts to and return back to your breath. Continue with this for a couple of minutes.

COME BACK: Start to engage with your physical senses. What sounds do you hear? Feel your weight in the chair and the soft pillow against your back. Can you recognize any scents? Visualize the scenery around you. When you've got a good grip on your senses, slowly open your eyes.

RECAP: Before you move a muscle, ask yourself how you're feeling. Are you calmer? Are you thinking more clearly? Feeling relaxed? Good! That's the goal. If you said no, that's fine. *It takes a little practice.*

Remember, meditation isn't for being present and giving your mind a breather. We can use it for a variety of things: to ponder ideas, find clarity, calm down, etc.

Meditation has been around for centuries, and there's a reason it's been around for this long and is growing in popularity: because it works. Staying consistent with your meditation practice will assist you in reaching a clear, calm state of mind so you may create space between your true beliefs and the thoughts and emotions that emerge, among other things. Meditation helps you get out of your head and out of your own way while you voyage closer toward your vision.

Take your time and cut yourself some slack with the learning process. Remember, meditation is a practice; you do not finish meditation, complete meditation, or win meditation. You *practice* meditation.

CHAPTER 9: GRATITUDE

Gratitude can have profound positive effects. It can boost our mood, change our outlook on life, and improve our overall well-being. With our spiritual wellness, gratitude is key.

We should take the time to connect with ourselves and our surroundings to understand how fortunate we are. Truthfully, our lives are filled with incredible things we fail to recognize every day.

Gratitude provides us with perspective. It's rather difficult to immerse ourselves into the realm of gratitude when there's ignorance involved. This ignorance usually blocks us from a new perspective we hadn't considered. Luckily, gratitude can help us overcome this ignorance, little by little, as it provides us with a bird's-eye view.

Can you think of a time when you were excessively frustrated when an emotion got the best of you? I'm sure you could—we've all been there. Let's say you missed the train, or maybe you received a low grade on an essay. Perhaps it's a little more extreme: Did you lose your job, intensely argue with your spouse, or break your cell phone?

Not to discredit the true inconvenience and frustration that can derive from these incidents, but while these scenarios can frustrate, they're not as catastrophic as they may seem when compared to the grand scheme of things.

Fortunately, jobs and cell phones are replaceable, and you and your spouse can always patch things up.

"Okay, what's your point?"

In 2019, the WHO and UNICEF confirmed that in 2017, globally, over 884 million people did not have access to clean water.[1]

Maybe you didn't hear me. 884 MILLION PEOPLE!

With that said, who are we to complain about the weather, missing the bus, or the guy driving 25 in the 30 when others lack basic necessities? Can you imagine not having access to clean water? What a nightmare. People are living this way daily.

We're so quick to show off our hardships. As if we were competing with one another in a cruel game of "who suffered more." Who knows why we do this—my guess is that people want respect or some justification after enduring hardship. Even though this may seem like the norm, which, unfortunately, it is, we cannot allow this concept to override us.

If we want to gain a better perspective, then we need to establish and pursue intentional pauses in our lives. We must provide ourselves with an opportunity to look around and observe from a higher viewpoint —a clearer perspective.

Far too often, we get caught up with things that, frankly, don't matter that much. Whether this is something out of our control, something from our past and any other frivolous worry you can think of, these sorts of things can keep us sidetracked.

Taking an intentional pause could be the first step to getting out of the awful repetitive cycle of concerning ourselves with things that genuinely don't matter that much. When we take time to pause, we create an opportunity to gauge the world around us and practice gratitude. We have a chance to consider the things we overlook daily.

Through the practice of gratitude, we can gain a clearer perspective. This is what gratitude is all about—finding clarity and becoming more appreciative in life; this helps us feel good, improve our health, savor our experiences, deal with adversity better, and build stronger and healthier relationships.[2]

When becoming more mindful of the things that do matter, start small. When we feel grateful for the small things in life, the larger things seem to be a bonus. Consider the things we often overlook—the air we breathe, the body we have, our family, our friends, etc.

"Well, how can I practice gratitude?"

Good question. There are a couple of practical ways.

First, we can practice gratitude through *journaling* (we'll actually dive deeper into journaling later). It's beneficial to physically write down the things we're grateful for. When we write our thoughts down on paper, we're able to see more clearly the things we overlook daily. This helps us recognize such things and become more appreciative of them.

When we journal, note whatever comes to mind when practicing gratitude, no matter how insignificant it may seem. With gratitude, it's easy to fall into the trap of writing down things we think we "should" be grateful for. For example, it seems more logical to be thankful for the oxygen we breathe than your little cup of coffee in the morning, right? Well, kind of.

Logically, it would make sense that oxygen is more significant than your coffee, but we're trying to write down what we're grateful for in the present moment. Don't complicate it. Write what comes to you.

Second, we can practice gratitude through *action*. We can find clarity and become more appreciative in life, which can provide us with numerous benefits. But we can create a deeper feeling of gratitude by sharing these perspectives with others.

We must utilize this positive energy we've harnessed via gratitude and put it back out into the universe. If we find ourselves fortunate enough to realize the importance of gratitude and even to practice it, then we must redistribute that energy back into the world for others.

Now, what does that mean? It means we redistribute the positive feelings that gratitude can bring us into the lives of others as best and as often as we can. More precisely, we're creating a positive ripple effect—which can last much longer than we anticipate.

Positive ripple effects transcend imagination, and all stem from one small act of kindness. The chain reaction you initiate can expand to people and places often far beyond our imagination. And typically, these ripple effects are created in instances overlooked.

There's a misconstrued idea that you need a large platform to make a difference. Well, I'm here to tell you that's simply not true. One person's actions could change the trajectory of another's whole life.

Think about it. If someone never introduced you to your first favorite book, you might not have eventually found your all-time favorite book. If your art teacher wasn't so great, you might have never picked up a brush.

If your friend never played soccer, you may have never been introduced to the sport you're so passionate about today.

Chances are when you think back on your own experiences similar to the ones listed above, it's likely that this person has no idea that they've sparked something in you. And believe it or not, you can do that for others, whether it's intentional or not.

This positive chain reaction lives on, and it may go unnoticed. Maybe you've introduced someone to the college that you attend, then they attend, and perhaps their kids and grandkids will want to attend too. If you show up to an open mic night after watching someone else get up there and do their thing, you may inspire someone in the crowd at that very moment. The possibilities are literally endless.

And there's no way to track this ripple effect in its entirety. It continues to expand and can travel vast distances and pass through significant lengths of time. And while it's difficult to track, it's easy to initiate.

Whether you're helping someone through hardship or calling them to say hello, the positivity you pass on to those who you come into contact with has no bounds. That "just because" phone call to your friend triggers a domino effect of positivity that dashes from the friend to another person, who then passes it to someone else, who passes it again and again. Person after person, the ripple effect continues.

While practicing gratitude is beneficial for our own sake, we should take the time to share this good feeling with others. It's important to distribute this energy often. And to do so, we must take action.

So, what are you waiting for? Call your parents, tell them how grateful you are for them. Text your friends and tell them you're hoping they have a wonderful day. Contact that old professor or teacher and let them know how they affected you. Hug your dog, tell a random person you like their outfit, or tell someone that their smile is contagious.

It doesn't matter how you put positive energy into the world, as long as you do it. Practice gratitude; gain a clearer perspective and add appreciation to your life. Once you've got your own fix, put positive energy out and begin this ripple effect. So, go ahead—make your contribution.

DIMENSION 2: PHYSICAL WELLNESS

Physical wellness is the act of taking care of your body to optimize your health condition and body function. It expands your knowledge about healthy living as well, which includes topics such as exercise, nutrition, and sleep.

There are many benefits to physical wellness, such as reducing the risk of heart disease, high cholesterol, and high blood pressure. Physical wellness can also boost your mood and energy levels and increase strength in bones, muscles, and joints. When your body is healthy, it will empower you to operate more efficiently in all aspects of life.[1]

Keeping a healthy quality of life is another way to get the most out of our days and life in general. With that, let's get right into it.

CHAPTER 10: FITNESS

"I regret exercising today," said no one ever. We all know that exercise is key to getting our bodies to a healthier state. It can help us prevent diseases, improve our sexual health, strengthen the body, and even help us live longer. Additionally, there is an abundance of research to support that physical exercise can lead to a healthier mind as well.[1]

Every time we exercise, our bodies release chemicals known as endorphins. These chemicals allow you to feel happy. The endorphins that are released during physical activity interact with the receptors in the brain that minimize your perception of pain.[2]

Have you heard of the runner's high? This is a state of euphoria that derives from a post-workout flow of endorphins.

Studies show that exercise also reduces levels of stress hormones in the body, such as adrenaline and cortisol.[3] Exercise even benefits our sleep. That's right—if your sleep schedule is disturbed by stress, depression, or anxiety, then exercise may help.[4]

Surely you knew some of this information already. But unless you've experienced this firsthand, you're on the outside looking in. There's a stronger connection between exercise and our quality of mind than you may think. On top of the benefits listed above, exercise can help you feel more comfortable in your own skin and allow you to feel better about yourself.

Think of your body as your own personal sculpture. Sure, it's not as easy to work on this sculpture, as it's a little more time-consuming than making something in your local sculpting class, but it's well worth it. Working on your personal fitness is invigorating as well as rewarding.

Now, there's no blueprint for personal fitness. In today's media, we're peppered with images and content from models, bodybuilders, and other people of this physical caliber. But these people have nothing to do with your own *fitness journey*. While they may look impressive, they symbolically represent the preconceived notions that tell us what we're "supposed" to look like. It's a little-known fact to those outside the fitness world that these images are more than false.

Your fitness journey is a personal journey. Sure, there's nothing wrong with wanting to look a certain way, as long as it's part of the vision you see for yourself. Just make sure it is suitable for you. Remember that there are many types of fitness, and people pursue these types for reasons other than aesthetics. I've outlined three popular types below.

First, there's *aerobic fitness*, which centers on conditioning your lungs and heart. Some may choose this fitness type because they simply enjoy it, wish to run marathons, or want to increase their stamina.

Next is *flexibility training*. This offers more freedom of movement and a more limber body. This training can be used for various reasons, such as to make day-to-day tasks easier or to reduce injuries.

Then there's *muscle strengthening*, which is precisely what it sounds like. It is typically associated with weight or resistance training.

"How do I know what to pick or do?"

Perhaps you're feeling lost in this part of the process. Thankfully, we live in an era where a quick search online can start you right away. So, search the internet. Research fitness in general as well as specific fitness types.

Identify your *fitness goals* (what you're looking to achieve or improve). Consider all aspects: How do you want to look and feel? What do you want to improve? Is there anything else that intrigues you? Read, watch, ask, and learn until you feel clear about what you want.

After you find something that interests you, explore the basics. You can find many videos and walkthroughs for beginners online.

Again, this is a personal journey; therefore, it's all subjective. Tailor your fitness goals to your specific wants and needs. This may include one particular fitness type or a combination of multiple fitness types.

From here, you can develop your *fitness vision*.

"How do I develop a fitness vision?"

Let's check it out.

FITNESS VISION

Begin by asking yourself questions about your fitness goals: What type of exercise intrigues you? What area of the body do you wish to improve upon? Is there a particular type of aesthetic you're going for?

Let's take a moment to visualize.

Tell me, what actions are you taking for yourself? Are you running early in the morning before sunrise? Maybe you're hitting the gym with your friends after work. Are you finding yourself feeling more energetic?

Whatever your vision looks like, make sure it is authentic. As you move through your fitness journey, you want to be reaching for goals important to you and you only. Be sure not to let a generic or outside perception of fitness alter your personal fitness goals or vision.

Now, once you've created a vision and considered what you'd like to do, you're ready to create your *fitness plan*.

FITNESS PLAN

"What does a fitness plan look like?"

A fitness plan, or should I say *your* fitness plan, should be customized for you and your personal schedule. Here are things to consider when creating your plan.

YOUR GOALS: Your fitness goals determine where you'll be going and what you'll be doing. These goals will help you decide what gym you'll join (if any), what equipment to get, and other similar things.

FREQUENCY: Figure out how often you're looking to exercise. Generally, a plan that most people follow when they begin is attempting to exercise 30 minutes a day, five days a week. But it's all subjective. Consider your fitness goals and personal schedule to execute your plan.

FUEL/RECOVERY: Consider the foods you'll need to keep yourself fueled and in good condition while recovering. We'll touch on nutrition in the next chapter, but as we mentioned, take time to do your research on not only your desired type of fitness and the basics but the type of diet that would best support this routine. If desired, consult a dietitian or nutritionist.

RESULTS: Rome wasn't built in a day like your dream body won't be built in a day. It takes some time to see results; slow your process down and do the work. In a few months, if you're not getting the results you want, change it up. Modify your diet, try a new exercise, increase the frequency of your workouts, or revisit your goals.

After you create a proper plan, you can then get to work.

While you work toward your fitness goals, you will attain a newfound sense of control. This sense of control will derive from the active decisions you make about the direction of your fitness journey. An additional quality you will obtain through this journey is *self-discipline*.

Learning to stay disciplined throughout your fitness journey will help you with your fitness goals and your goals outside of the fitness realm. The perseverance and patience you will obtain while aiming for these goals will translate well into other areas of your life. Through this process, you will allow yourself to become more confident and tenacious.

The self-discipline you will use in your fitness journey will help develop your mental fortitude. Motivation will not cover you each day, and this is where discipline drops in. Discipline is there to guide you when motivation needs a break.

You can also reinforce self-discipline through your vision. You must paint a mental picture so you may know what you're potentially giving up on days you think about not putting in the work; this is one reason that creating a vision is so important. You can *want* this vision more than anything, but first, you must deem yourself *willing*. If you are unwilling to get up and take steps toward your goals, then nothing will get done.

As you check off your goals, you will tally up personal accolades that will help fuel you on this journey and provide you with a refreshing feeling of accomplishment. Personal fitness will offer the opportunity to set both short-term and long-term goals, which will bring a sense of pride.

Before we close out, let's summarize. We are looking to:

- Research fitness and explore specific fitness types.
- Identify fitness goals.
- Create a fitness vision.
- Develop a fitness plan.

So, what're you waiting for? Get after it! Take time and complete the steps above and begin your fitness journey. Soon enough, you will realize that you are becoming the master of your own self and that you are in control of how you further your fitness journey while reaping the significant health benefits that come along with it.

CHAPTER 11: NUTRITION

Exercise has a sibling, better known as nutrition. Plenty of fitness gurus will tell you that getting up and doing an hour of exercise is the easy part. The hard part is controlling what goes on your plate for the next 23 hours. No ignorance here; this act can be difficult.

As one unhealthy meal doesn't make you unhealthy, one healthy meal doesn't make you healthy. It's all about consistency. It's hard to stay consistent with a healthy diet, as, most of the time, it's not always prepared, isn't as flavorful, and is relatively more expensive. Believe it or not, this is all for a reason.

Do you know why healthy food is more expensive? Or why supplement shops flourish with their new, overpriced supplement product? Well, the people who rave about these things understand one thing: *it's healthy*.

Essentially, others are so willing to pay high prices for things like this because they understand the benefits of a healthy lifestyle. Healthy food in our body offers a variety of benefits, including better-looking skin, stronger bones and muscles, a healthier digestive system, and life longevity.[1]

When considering these outcomes, there's no wonder people are paying extra to get in on the act. I'm sure you know many people who claim to know this but perhaps don't buy into healthy eating's degree of success or noticeability. We'll get to this.

"So you're saying healthy food leads to overall better health? Sounds pretty obvious. Didn't we already know that?"

You probably did. But what I'm pointing out is the importance of recognizing and being mindful of how accessible and affordable unhealthy food is and what it can actually do to our bodies.

Fried food is easily accessible and available at most restaurants. French fries, mozzarella sticks, chicken nuggets, and other similar foods are typical foods you'd find nearly anywhere and are relatively affordable. While this may seem like the norm, it is not. These foods can increase heart disease risk and can be detrimental to your overall health.[2] But today, they are often a regular part of a meal. *Don't be fooled.*

Take some time in the next day or two to notice the foods being advertised and how often you see these ads.

"Okay, thanks for the public health scare. What're you saying?"

Today, businesses will wave mass amounts of unhealthy food under our noses, and we're okay with that. Because it is normalized, we're ignorant of its effects on us. Because we consider these foods to be ordinary, we never question their effects.

Unfortunately, due to its lack of emphasis, it's difficult for people to understand why eating healthy is important. There's usually a claim after someone's failed two-week bender of eating healthy stating it changed nothing. Apparently, a plethora of people do not maintain healthy lifestyles long enough to see the effects on the body. Fortunately for you, you're reading this information now. So, let's jump right into it, shall we?

A steady diet of healthy food can assist our neurotransmitter production. We are setting ourselves up for an overall happier mood, improved focus, and fewer mood fluctuations when we provide our stomachs with healthier foods.[3] Do you recall the "second brain" topic from earlier?

As you may recall, the enteric nervous system (ENS) is a collection of brain-like neurons and neurotransmitters in our stomachs, and many researchers claim that an unhealthy digestive system is strongly linked to neurological and mental health issues.

Ah, yes. See how things come full circle? We must take care of that second brain!

There are *good* and *bad* types of bacteria that enter our stomachs. An example of a beneficial or *good* type of bacteria is bifidobacteria, which helps provide anti-aging effects, prevent intestinal inflammation, and enhance overall gut health.

Low counts of bifidobacteria are linked to plenty of diseases. While bifidobacteria supplements may help treat specific disease symptoms, studies have shown that people with obesity, diabetes, and allergic asthma, among other health issues, appear to have lower levels of bifidobacteria in their intestines than healthy people. Bifidobacteria levels can be increased by ingesting specific foods and drinks such as green tea, apples, berries, and onions.[4]

Researchers have discovered nearly 50 species of beneficial bacteria, each of which can provide us with positive health benefits. Non-beneficial or *bad* bacteria can cause an array of issues, such as irritable bowel syndrome, constipation, heartburn, bloating, unexplained weight gain or loss, sleep disturbance, and skin irritation.[5]

Many foods, such as highly processed food and alcohol, can have a negative impact on gut bacteria. Sugar is also a key culprit. That's right—excessive sugar intake can cause too many bad bacteria to form in our gut and lead to inflammation.[6]

Too much sugar in our system can cause an alternating spike in our mood. When we intake lots of sugar, we get fleeting "feel-good" neurotransmissions that are followed by a crash. When we do this often, we believe that these things we do to our bodies are "normal," and we may continue to sabotage our health unknowingly.[7]

And that is precisely my point. Guided by the "traditional" way of doing things, we are *unknowingly sabotaging our health*. We are predisposed to believe that consuming foods that cause negative effects on our bodies (fried food, fast food, excessive sugar) is normal. We must note this and regulate our diets.

If you're looking to improve your overall physical health, nutrition is the way. When you maintain a healthier diet and eat more mindfully, you can drastically improve your overall well-being.

Don't overlook this idea. Remember, exercise is a major piece of the puzzle, but again, the most difficult bout is controlling what goes on your plate in the 23 hours that follow. What's wonderful is this is something you can alter right now. So go change that grocery list!

Have fun with this opportunity and build that better you—today.

CHAPTER 12: SLEEP

If you're looking to get serious about your health, then you have to get serious about sleep. Believe it or not, sleep is as important to our health as our diet. Poor sleep is linked to physical problems such as a weakened immune system, and it can also affect our mental health by contributing to issues such as anxiety and depression.[1]

With effort, we can find ways to sleep more efficiently, soundly, and restfully. A ton of benefits derive from getting good quality sleep. Sleep can boost our immune system, enhance our mood, increase productivity, and improve memory, among other things.[2]

"How can we improve our sleep?"

First, we must view sleep as a priority.

Sleep is essential to being human. We spend a third of our lives asleep. We can't survive without it, and the better we sleep, the more efficiently we can operate.

Not getting enough sleep may result in an overall negative mood and facilitate irritability and poor concentration. These contribute to anxiety and depression. In addition, going for too long without quality sleep offers similar effects to intoxication, leading to poor judgment and performance.[3]

When we understand the importance of sleep, we can make it more of a priority in our lives. From here, we can take strides to improve our overall *sleep hygiene*—which can be improved by choosing new tactics to implement.

Start with developing a nighttime routine. Now, let's get one thing straight: developing a nighttime routine can be easy—but executing this routine and staying consistent with it is a whole different game. We must become mindful in this department.

"What does an ideal nighttime routine actually look like?"

While a nighttime routine should be tailored to your specific liking, there are a few key tactics to consider.

But before we get to the routine nighttime tactics, identify a specific bedtime to help regulate this schedule—ideally, something that covers seven to eight hours of sleep. From here, we'll note a few tactics you may want to put into action before this designated bedtime. Once you've chosen a few tactics to weave into your new or existing nighttime routine, you'll now be better able to gauge how long this nighttime routine will take.

Let's check out these tactics.

First, to improve your sleep quality, reduce your blue light exposure come nightfall. Blue light is a color in the visible light spectrum. It has a short wavelength, which means it creates higher amounts of energy.[4]

All electromagnetic radiation is characterized by wavelength. These wavelengths are defined by size. The longer the wavelength, the less energy it carries. The shorter the wavelength, the more energy it carries. Blue and violet light have the highest energy in the visible light spectrum, which can be damaging to our eyes.

We receive blue light from things such as the sun and the screens of our digital devices. Blue light stimulates parts of our brain that can make us feel awake and alert.[5] Obviously, this can be helpful during the day, but quite the opposite at night.

We should reduce the screen time we use at night to help us grow tired faster. Try turning your phone off an hour before bed and keeping it off until the morning. I know, I know, I'm asking a lot of you. All I'm saying is, try it. For a few nights, turn your phone off and cut the urge to check your phone every five minutes. After a few nights of good sleep, you'll see the bigger picture.

One of the most valuable parts of a nighttime routine is taking the time to wind down. The way we go about this is subjective, but common activities include meditating, journaling, reading, listening to music, or taking a hot shower. Spending just 10 minutes doing a wind-down exercise may allow for noticeable improvements in your sleep quality. Find something that will enable you to relax, both mentally and physically.

Now, let's touch on the act of sleeping. After our routine is done, it's time for bed. Let's keep that momentum going by creating an ideal sleep environment for yourself. Keep the room dark and cool. Light exposure can disturb our sleeping patterns, so block those windows. Additionally, cooler temperatures have been linked to deeper sleep as it helps our bodies reach a lower core temperature faster. When our core temperature drops, that's when sleepiness can occur.[6]

Take time to develop this schedule. Tailor it to you and you only and go out of your way to help yourself. Fuel your ambition to complete your nighttime schedule and improve your sleep hygiene by continuing to view sleep as a priority—all facts considered, it has proven itself to be one.

Let's summarize. Our new nighttime routine may consist of:

- Choosing a *strict* designated bedtime.
- Reducing blue light usage.
- Practicing wind-down activities.
- Creating an ideal sleeping environment.

Now that we've identified steps you can take to improve sleep, it's time to put these things into action. There's no better time to start than now. Sleep tight!

DIMENSION 3: EMOTIONAL WELLNESS

Emotional wellness is a person's ability to handle the emotions presented in life. It's about being mindful, understanding, and accepting of these emotions and managing them effectively. When we can manage our feelings properly, we can maneuver through life's challenges and stressful moments with a little more ease.

Emotional wellness also includes weaving activities into our lifestyle, such as journaling and practicing positivity, to allow for clarity and understanding. With effort, emotional wellness will help us become more comfortable with ourselves, more adaptive, more resilient, and better communicators.

CHAPTER 13: JOURNALING

When we find ourselves in a stressful rut, it can be hard to pull ourselves out. At times, it feels like we're stuck at a crossroads; we feel lost and don't know which direction to head. It's hard to deliberate as we feel there are a million options to carefully consider before our next move.

A typical reason for this rut is we're either pushing our energy in the wrong direction or simply ignoring it in hopes of the rut disappearing. So, where do we go from here? Well, journaling is a great go-to tactic for clearing the mind.

Journals are home to authenticity; they're the place where our truth shines. Our most authentic self can be written and even realized on these pages of paper. Journaling provides an opportunity to be transparent with no immediate judgment. It can help us alleviate stress, collect our thoughts, clear our minds, create new ideas, recognize patterns, and express ourselves.

Now, I know what you're thinking. "Journaling? Like, writing in a diary?" Well, yeah—but instead of writing about your sixth-grade crush, you're using it to help create some space in your mind.

When you're caught up with everyday life, it's challenging to make sense of and grasp everything going on in your mind. When you journal, you put your thoughts to paper, thus making them more apprehensible. It's a more linear way of thinking.

Concealing our problems is a significant reason for mental clutter. When our stress levels are high, we must find relief. For some, it's exercise. For others, it's chatting with a friend or finding some quiet time to relax. Some people choose to journal as it's a more convenient and accessible way to ditch some of that stress.

Keep a small journal nearby to release some of that clutter by jotting down a few lines about how you feel. Allowing your stress to fester won't help you; try writing these thoughts down to get them out of your mind.

According to Maud Purcell, a psychotherapist and an expert on journaling, we're engaging the left side of our brain when we journal. This side of our brain is rational and analytical. So, while the left side of your brain is busy participating in writing, the right side of your brain is doing what it does best, being creative.[1]

The right side of your brain is being intuitive, creative, and feeling, while the left side of your brain is occupied because you're writing, thus removing mental blocks and allowing you to write your authentic beliefs onto paper without the resistance of rational and analytical thinking.[2]

In other words, your emotional self is shining through. We can use journaling as a tool to better understand ourselves and unload our cluttered minds when we need to.

"What sort of things should I journal about?"

We are coming full circle here. While there's an abundance of prompts you could use, consider gratitude. Practicing gratitude is an incredible way to shift our mindset into a more positive state. Reminding ourselves of everything we are grateful for will open up the floodgates for this thinking to occur more consistently. We're attracting similar behaviors, observations, and thinking processes that come along with expressing gratitude.

I'd recommend taking the time to do this right when you wake up, right before you go to sleep, or at both times. It does not need to be a demanding exercise that requires a lot of writing or time. If you're in a rush, take a quick minute. The end goal is to make journaling part of your routine, so find the time.

All things considered, the act of journaling has something to offer, and there's something for everyone. There are endless prompts for you, whether you're designing them for yourself or discovering new ones online to use.

Aside from gratitude, here are a few other prompts you could try:

- Brain dump (writing out all of your thoughts).
- Write out your accomplishments.
- List the best parts of your day.
- Identify short-term and long-term goals.
- Write a message to yourself to read on bad days.
- Create a bucket list.

Try to make your journal time something to look forward to. Incorporate it into your daily cup of coffee or into your nighttime routine. Associate journaling with one of your most relaxing and enjoyable activities to keep it consistent.

The next time your world feels chaotic, turn to journaling. It's a therapeutic way to blow off steam and get those pesky thoughts out of your mind and onto the page. Utilize this helpful outlet as often as necessary and watch your stress melt away.

CHAPTER 14: POSITIVITY

Positivity is wonderful. What's not to like? It feels great, it sounds great— it is *great*. We love to surround ourselves with positivity, be around positive people, and take positive actions. But like anything else, too much of it can be a bad thing.

Hey, don't get me wrong, positivity is great. And to be blunt, most of us don't have enough positivity in our lives. It's crucial that we add more of it into our daily routine—and don't worry, we'll get to that. But what I'm getting at is that having an *extreme* fixation on positivity may actually hurt us in the long run.

This is known as "toxic positivity." It's an overgeneralization of an optimistic mind-state that ultimately ends with neglect of the human experience.[1] In other words, it may cause us to ignore and deny our negative emotions.

Earlier we noted that our emotions are temporary experiences that are a part of the human experience. Trying to suppress them will only allow them to come back stronger. Learning to observe, accept, and let go of these emotions is the key to not letting them have control over you. You must acknowledge these feelings and remind yourself that they don't have control over you.

Resisting all negativity will cloud our judgment and allow us to get hurt more easily. If we try to completely cut out negativity, then any reality check will put us out of commission. We will unknowingly encase our ego in a fragile bubble that can be damaged far too easily.

And sure enough, we'll try to protect this bubble. We may avoid family, friends, and anyone who may have the slightest bit of negative news to share. We may accidentally place ourselves in an isolated box, one where we think everyone is negative and we're the only sane ones. This leads to loneliness, which leads to sadness.

Now, I'm not saying we should surround ourselves with negative people. I'm saying that if we adopt a toxic positivity lifestyle, we'll build up a weak, overly sensitive defense mechanism against these inevitable negative people and situations.

Instead of blocking it out, I suggest we learn to embrace negativity and accept it as a feature of human existence. Do you recall from earlier in this book that negativity acts as a defense mechanism? It's a part of being human.

The bottom line is this: everything can't be positive all the time. I mean, sure, a stress-free life without an ounce of negativity in sight sounds lovely, but is it really?

I pose a theory: if everything were only positive in some miraculous way, life would be pretty stale.

Think about it. What would we consider good if everything was the same? How would we differentiate things? What would make us an individual? How would we decide what we like? How could we tell two people apart? The list goes on and on.

If there were only positivity, then everything would have to be positive to the same degree to fulfill the idea that there can be no lack—no negative aspects of one specific thing or anything. This would leave life as a stale, boring, and stagnant loop.

So, you see, we actually need the opposition. Negativity is required. How could we desire anything if everything was the same? The answer is that we couldn't—simply because there would be no difference between anything at all. So, what would be the point?

Positivity and negativity—it's yin and yang.

There can be no yin without the yang, as they allow for differentiation. A polar opposite force is needed in all things. Without it, there would be nothing. The yin-yang concept demonstrates that, quite literally, nothing can exist without its opposite.

Yin-yang also shows us that balance is key. Yin and yang exist in harmony—they need each other to create a balance. The mix of both the positive and the negative, is what makes up this thing called life. They are interdependent—one can't exist without the other.

"Yeah, that's cool and all, but what are you getting at?"

Okay, what I'm poking at is twofold.

First, trying to be *only* positive is toxic positivity at work. Ironically, *too much* positivity may leave us disconnected from others who are embracing all of life's emotions. In society today, we've come to believe that a steady positive emotional state is our default human setting, which is simply not true. As humans, we'll encounter many emotions—as there is a range to be experienced.

Second, negativity allows for positivity to shine; without one, the other doesn't exist, so embrace them both to fully experience life.

However, it may be wise to consider this: positivity should be sprinkled into our daily lives and not forced upon us under the guise that it is our default setting.

When we try to gently weave more positivity into our lives, we may see more substantial results than if we attempt to *force* an excessive number of positive behaviors and practices into our everyday lives.

Remember, if we overemphasize positivity, we could become fixated and overly analytic about it. As we talked about in the law of attraction chapter, if we think about something too much, we inadvertently focus on its lack, which gives us an unsatisfying result that opposes our original intent.

We should find bite-sized ways to weave more positivity into our lives. It's a more practical approach than forcefully attempting to become exclusively positive and completely rid our lives of negativity. The goal is to add more positivity to the equation, not to subtract negativity entirely from it.

"How do I practice positivity?"

There are a plethora of ways you can practice positivity, a few of which are already listed in this book. Try some of these!

AFFIRMATIONS: One way to practice positivity is to create an affirmation tailored to you. Recite this affirmation often. Write it on a sticky note and post it on your fridge, bathroom mirror, car, office, or anywhere you'd like. Take this a step further and find your own creative ways to remind yourself to use your custom affirmation daily.

START YOUR DAY ON A POSITIVE NOTE: Whether with exercise, a quick meditation, a fun journal prompt, some gratitude, or anything you'd like, doing something positive for yourself in the morning is a superb way to start your day and set the tone for the remainder of the day.

CONSUME POSITIVE MEDIA: Pick up positive books, listen to positive speakers, or listen to positive music. Gauge your daily media intake: if your social media is bombarded with negativity or things you'd rather not see, then take time to filter out anything deemed unnecessary.

That ex-boyfriend you haven't seen in years—unfollow. That negative coworker who's still bitching about his job—unfollow. Get rid of negative people from your social network and replace them with different types of positive media you can access throughout your day.

REFRAME NEGATIVE THOUGHTS: It's foolish to expect we'll never have a negative thought again. That's just silly. Remember, our brains are hardwired for negativity as a defense mechanism. With that said, when we become mindful of what negative thoughts actually are and why we have them, then we can stop resisting them so much. From there, we can replace them with positive thoughts.

When a negative thought arrives, be intuitive. You know your true self. Don't let your worry and inhibition override your intuition. Swap the negative thought with a positive thought you know is authentic.

Swapping negative thoughts with positive ones may feel a little inauthentic at first, but that's okay. Keep going. Emphasize the positive thoughts you want to have. They're not inauthentic if these are thoughts you genuinely wish to have present.

Inauthentic thoughts are what make you frustrated; a clear indication that they are unwanted and not crafted by your true self. Negative thoughts are not you, as you are not them. They are *just* thoughts; that is all. They are nonsense, and they *cannot* hurt you and they do *not* control you.

Remember, you can't suppress these thoughts or try to get rid of them completely, as that will only allow them to come back stronger. Instead, look to challenge them *only* when it feels necessary—you don't want to challenge every damn thought that comes to mind. Some thoughts you may disregard altogether as you understand how foolish they are.

And that's the goal: to realize how silly and nonsensical these negative thoughts are. After you challenge and disregard these negative thoughts, eventually, you will see how unnecessary it is to even entertain them in the first place.

SURROUND YOURSELF WITH POSITIVE PEOPLE: If you have friends, family, or acquaintances who bring you peace or lighten your mood, make time to see them. Suggest meeting up more often for coffee or taking time to message them sometimes. Surround yourself with positive people and notice how it alters your mood for the better.

TREAT YOURSELF AS YOU WOULD TREAT A FRIEND: If a friend came to you with a problem, you wouldn't sit there and help them beat themselves up over it, would you? Of course not. So, why would you do the same to yourself?

Practice self-compassion and be kind to yourself. Did you make a mistake? Welcome to the club. Now learn from it and move forward. Become mindful of how you're speaking to yourself in these instances and change the narrative.

Note the quality of your self-talk. If you find that you're not as friendly or supportive to yourself as you'd like, then adjust.

CUT YOURSELF SOME SLACK ONCE IN A WHILE: You're not perfect—no one is. So, stop trying to be. If you're trying your best, then what more can you do?

If you're feeling like you're making progress, then praise yourself once in a while. Continue moving in a positive direction, and you will only continue to grow.

Give these tactics a try and throw more positivity into your daily life; you deserve it. Try them all and see which ones work best for you. One may be your thing, another may not, and that's fine. Continue to search for other (and possibly more helpful) tactics for practicing positivity until you find a system that suits you well.

DIMENSION 4: SOCIAL WELLNESS

Social wellness refers to our relationships and how we interact with those around us. It is creating and nurturing relationships in all facets of life.[1] While it's one of four dimensions of wellness, which are all significant, this one seems to be the most overlooked. So, let's take some time and chat about social health, its importance, and how we can obtain better social health in our own lives.

CHAPTER 15: SOCIAL HEALTH

As human beings, we are naturally social. It's quite literally hardwired into our brains. We're interested in what's going on around us. We're fixated on what other people are up to, what someone may think or say about this or that, who did this, who said what, and so on.

These social tendencies have developed and adapted throughout human history, ultimately leading to this very day, where we've evolved into hyper-social beings. Being social is a part of being human, so much so our brains show signs of social activity before we can even walk.

As infants, we're already participating in social connections—typically with our parents or caregivers—through something called "attachment distress." This is a social concept where infants become aware of their needs and, as they begin to understand that only their caregiver can provide such needs, they become attached to the caregiver. Intense interconnectedness forms between the parties; more than meets the eye.

Infants have an attachment system. Its purpose is to monitor our parents' or caregivers' proximity to keep us safe. When infants feel the distance has gotten too far for their liking, their bodies set off an alarm. This alarm comes to the surface as crying, which signals the parents or caregivers to return to a closer distance.

We're all born with this attachment system, and it lives within us our whole lives. This is the reason for our intense need to be social: it's our human nature. Being social is not a want—it's a human need.[1]

So, you see, we are naturally social beings from the jump—long before we can even conceptualize what it means to be social.

But even in our current, more developed state of being, social health is important. The ways we interact in our social world can alter our biochemistry just as much as the food we consume does, as each interaction will cause different hormonal reactions in our bodies.

Our bodies act as a roller coaster as we maneuver our social experiences, full of highs and lows of hormones and emotional reactions. Some of these affect us positively, while others affect us negatively. So, to keep the sensations in our body a bit more pleasurable and our experiences on the positive side, we should pay close attention and acknowledge the importance of our social health.

"What is social health exactly?"

Closely linked to social wellness, "social health" refers to our ability to interact and form meaningful relationships with those around us.[2] Social health concerns gauging your current social life and understanding whether or not there is a need for adjustment. Let's try it.

Take a moment to consider your relationships. Are your relationships, or perhaps your general lack of relationships, affecting you in other areas of life? For example, is that asshole boss of yours negatively affecting the downtime with your spouse? Suppose you find that your relationships, or lack of relationships, negatively affect other areas of your life. This is a sign you may need to adjust to improve your social health.

Let's dive deeper into the importance of social health.

If I asked you, "What is your most painful memory?" how would you respond? Probably with a story about a breakup, losing a loved one, an embarrassing moment, a divorce, an intense argument with a friend or family member, or something similar, no?

It's likely that most of us would overlook talking about a physical wound and would instead mention a time when we experienced a "social wound." Did you know that we actually remember our social pain more than our physical pain? That's right; we're more prone to recalling a tough social situation than a physical injury.

If you're wondering why, the simple answer is this: physical and social pain are not that different from each other. Research shows that social pain activates the same brain regions as physical pain. They both utilize the same neural pathways, which makes it impossible for us to feel them simultaneously.[3]

Although we don't take it as seriously, social pain is as real as physical pain.

Physical pain is less physical than it is believed to be. Now, I'm not claiming that physical pain is all in your head, but there are psychological aspects of physical pain to consider.

Take the placebo effect, for instance. It's the classic sugar pill tale. Let's say an individual is aching from a particular activity and visits a doctor who then prescribes them a pill, claiming this will offer pain relief. This pill is simply a sugar pill—there's nothing in it that would help this individual.

But miraculously, it works. How could this be? Well, it's because this individual believed that the pill would help them. Do you recall our friend Emile Coué and the concept of affirmations? Ah yes, it's all coming together.

This concept works because we associate pain relief with taking the pill. Similarly, placebo studies have shown numerous health benefits, including an increased production of endorphins.[4] All of this considered, it's apparent that social pain can leave as much of an imprint as physical pain.

"Okay, and your point?"

My point is our social health is not only vital but overlooked. We're quick to protect ourselves from physical pain, while we neglect to protect ourselves from social pain. Valuing and maintaining your social health is crucial to achieving overall wellness in life.

Widening our social circles and creating meaningful connections with others can be immensely beneficial. It can increase overall happiness, help us create a sense of belonging, sharpen our cognitive skills, and even help us live longer.[5]

In Japan, the most prominent location for centenarians (individuals aged 100 or older), it's evident that social interaction is a major factor in their lifestyle choices, which contributes to their longevity. According to the international bestseller, *Ikigai*, a book about Japanese secrets that lead to a long and happy life, socialization can significantly affect our lifespan.

In this inspiring book, authors Héctor García and Francesc Miralles cross-compare data from various centenarians to find that social interaction, more specifically karaoke time spent with friends, is a recurring trend found in the habits and lifestyles of these long-lived individuals.

García and Miralles conducted 100 interviews with Japanese centenarians and compiled a list of similarities among all interviewees. The interviews contained questions about the centenarians' personal philosophies, their *ikigai* (reason for being), and their secrets to longevity.

Key social aspects for centenarians were: They all belonged to some neighborhood association, where they felt cared for by others. They all held a powerful sense of community as they helped each other with everything, from working out in the fields to building houses to helping with municipal projects.[6]

Along with the science-backed evidence provided, these centenarians stand as living proof to support the importance of social health: strong social ties and a sense of community significantly contribute to one's longevity.

"Okay, you've sold me. So, how do we tend to our social health?"

Great question. There are plenty of ways to improve our social health. Thankfully, I had the opportunity to speak with an expert on the subject.

Introducing Dr. Chelsea Shields: American bio-social anthropologist, placebo studies expert, human evolution expert, strategic consultant, women's rights activist, TED Fellow, and holder of dual PhDs in biological anthropology and cultural anthropology.

Dr. Shields' passion for anthropology shone brightly throughout our series of insightful conversations. We discussed the current state of social health and whether or not we're becoming less social as a species. Dr. Shields explained that we're still connected, but it's in a contradictory way. Today, social media keeps us connected. But in an era where we're the most connected we've ever been as a society, we're also the most lonely.

How can this be? Because of less in-person community interaction, as it's easier to connect via social media platforms, we're becoming more independent in our daily lives. It's as if we love having fewer commitments and seemingly limitless freedom. But, with this approach, we opt out of discomfort, as it's more comfortable to converse with others from behind a screen. Ironically, this hurts us in the long run.

The accessibility and convenience of using social media offer the façade of connectivity. What's more, the overbearingness of social media platforms make us feel not only disconnected but lost in translation.

We're overstimulated as a collection of friends, family, and people we hardly know post their best moments on social media. We're becoming overexposed. We see everyone's highlights through the lens of social media and, over time, are left believing we are lacking.

At the same time, we're drowning in a sea of opinions. Social media platforms give people a voice, which is great, but being inundated with an excessive number of opinions from the millions of platform users leaves us feeling small as if our voice does not matter as much as others. Social media will have you buy into this foolish idea. Do not fall into the trap.

As we continued on the topic, Dr. Shields made it clear that we desperately need real social interaction, now more than ever.

SOCIAL HEALTH TACTICS

In our conversations, Dr. Shields offered useful tactics to improve our social health.

First, she emphasized that everyone needs at least one emotional support human. Whether this is a best friend, a close family member, a therapist, or anything between, finding someone we can share with and confide in is paramount.

Second, we must determine our internal feelings when around others. We should base this on our own levels of joy. The next time you're with someone or a group of others, ask yourself how you're feeling. If you notice resistance or any inhibition, consider distancing yourself. But, if you find these individuals or groups of others genuinely bring you joy, spend more time with them.

Third, ask yourself: Is the person I'm around someone I'd want to be like? Well, are they? You're likely to become more like those you surround yourself with. So, make sure your social circle contains individuals who make you feel important and loved and who inspire you.

Last, increase your level of confidence. While confidence can help us do various things, like boost our self-esteem, it can also assist us in the social world. Most of our communication comes from non-verbal cues, and how we carry ourselves can draw in others who wish to mimic our energy levels. Remember, like attracts like. So, use this tactic to draw in those whose energy you'd enjoy and perhaps benefit from.

The quality of our wellness relies heavily on the quality of our social health. We call it social "health" for a reason. According to a *Washington*

Post article, a former surgeon general explains that social isolation can be as harmful to your health as smoking 15 cigarettes a day.[7] This is nothing to play with lightly. We must understand the importance of social health and tend to it when needed.

Dr. Shields does an excellent job of highlighting the significance of social health in our lives, and in one of her many exceptional TED Talks, she reached a crescendo with this closing bit of insight: having a healthy social life won't only determine how happy you are, but also how *healthy* you are.[8]

PART III — ACTION

Action is the glue that holds everything together. It bridges the gap between where we are and where we want to be. Without action, nothing will get done and everything will remain the same. One way we can take action—and continue to do so—is through creating habits.

Let's get down to business.

CHAPTER 16: BUILDING HABITS

Success is not linear. There is no consistent upward trajectory toward a goal without some hiccups along the way. Generally, outsiders will only see the final product or outcome.

They will assume it's an overnight success without understanding how much work went on behind the scenes. But there's no such thing as an overnight success—at least, I've never seen one. Primarily, success stems from consistency in good habits.

Consistency brings us closer to completing a goal or obtaining lasting change. We often overlook small changes because we believe that big success requires big change. In reality, however, this is not usually the case.

Most people hold the belief we must struggle and take on massive responsibility to break into mainstream success. We believe we must move mountains to have the success that is "real." But while some are waiting for lightning, others are improving daily.

Habits can make or break our chances of achieving our goals. It's all about compounding smaller habits to equal success in the long term. Habits are a major factor in the equation for success, as thoughtful routines can provide a clearer and smoother path to our goals.

We live in a fast-paced society. With our phones, everything is at our fingertips, ready instantaneously, from grocery delivery to ridesharing. But when reaching for our goals, things may take longer than we'd like. Results don't seem to come fast enough for us.

The progress we're making is usually a slower process than we prefer. Time and consistency are the primary contributors to real and lasting change—they're the two elements vital to success in the long term.

"Well, what about epiphanies? Or something drastic that gives us a sudden realization to change?"

Before we dive in, let's get this out of the way now: epiphanies are overrated and overestimated. Many believe that you need a rock-bottom story or a wild, thought-provoking realization to change your behaviors or narrative. This is not entirely true.

While grand realizations can help put us on the route to success, the need for a dramatic introduction to your newfound path toward success is not necessary. Your life is not a Broadway play.

We change because we *decide* to change. Simple as that. There's not always a specific defining moment to propel us into a new life or lifestyle. Just because we have a significant realization doesn't mean we're required to act on it. We make a choice to act.

Again, these breakthrough glimpses of success do not come overnight—we must work for them. These moments come from a series of small wins and progress over time through consistency. Thus, *learning to build consistent habits* is what will ultimately bring about lasting change, significant progress, and goal achievement.

"Well, what about motivation? Isn't this a major factor in creating new habits and obtaining our goals?"

Motivation alone will benefit short-term goals more than long-term goals.

Motivation is a piece of the puzzle, but it's only a single piece. Relying on motivation in the long term is a trap; you're setting yourself up for failure.

Motivation comes and goes. We could receive bursts of it one day and find it missing the next. It's easy to fall into the motivation trap, believing that motivation on its own will help us execute our goals in the long term. This idea is a hamster wheel. Often, we think that "this time" we've got the motivation formula nailed down, which will help us keep our habits. Don't fall for it.

Learn to be reflective in these instances. We should look back and ask ourselves: How many times did we attempt this change with just motivation as fuel? And, how many times did it work?

"So, how do we actually initiate new habits?"

It may be more helpful to lead with some forethought before taking some action.

First, *be specific*. We must identify what it is we're looking to accomplish. "I will exercise more this week" is not specific enough. Instead, "I will work out on this day at this time for this long" is more precise and more likely to keep you locked in. Otherwise, you may push your goal off. Next thing you know, you didn't get to it.

It's far less challenging to set and accomplish the goals *we want*—so decide what those goals are. Write them down, put them out into the universe, and put in the work.

Second, *set reasonable expectations*—don't overwhelm yourself. All too often, we bite off more than we can chew. For example, let's say there's

125

something that motivates us, then we set overly high (at the time, seemingly doable) expectations, follow the routines and habits for a week, then we steadily decline back to square one. So, what happened?

We've jumped the gun. We set unrealistic expectations for ourselves, which we couldn't keep up with. Now, it's important to remember that this is not your fault. You do not lack motivation, discipline, or the determination to keep new habits; you simply utilized a common approach that rarely works as it's too overwhelming.

You must build your way up. Keep acting on small habits easily done with low motivation until you decide it's time to level up and maintain more difficult habits. Don't set unrealistic expectations for yourself. For example, don't say you'll run for an hour every day and not be able to stick to it. Start small.

Set the bar lower. I'm not saying you shouldn't strive for bigger and better things—I'm saying you should work at it. Keep your base solid and stay consistent when trying to create lasting change. Lay down bricks to build your foundation, not another house of cards.

Once we've identified our specific goals and have set reasonable expectations, it's time to set up *habit prompts*. Let's chat about two primary ideas we can use to help ourselves begin and maintain our new habits.

HABIT ACCESSIBILITY

A great way to begin and keep a new habit is by making it easily accessible. For example, if you're looking to read more often, carry your book with you wherever you go. Find opportunities to read at work, between classes, during your lunchtime, anywhere and anytime.

Keep your habits visible. The bike you've wanted to use more will not get much use if it's collecting dust in your crowded basement. Make it apparent. Put these things in plain sight for easy access. The more accessible the habit is, the more likely it will occur.

The same goes for our bad habits. Sick of using social media? Delete the apps! Are you tired of spending too much time watching TV? Unplug it! Want to stop eating unhealthy food? Don't keep it around! Rid these things from your atmosphere and free from easy access.

The easier a habit is, the more likely we are to engage in it. Remember, large influxes of motivation are not always readily available. It simply comes and goes. If you find motivation levels are low, but your habit is easily accessible, then you're still likely to act on the habit.

HABIT TERRITORY

Another idea is to find a specific territory for a habit. Now, while habit accessibility is important to consider, the accessibility factor may render it useless if you are placed in a poor environment for these new habits to occur. If so, consider creating a new habit territory.

We *already* have unconscious territories for specific habits.[1] For example, perhaps your bedroom is strictly for sleeping and relaxing; let's say this is the *only* room you do each of these activities in your house. Therefore, you associate sleep and relaxation with your bedroom. If so, would it be ideal to do three taxing hours of homework in this space? Probably not.

Creating territories for habits to occur in is vital to begin new habits without getting caught up in our old ones. For example, if you're looking to read more, you're less likely to get that done in the living room with four screaming kids instead of a designated quiet space for reading.

Identify specific territories for habits to help with habit execution. Perhaps you will have a work territory, a reading territory, a relaxing territory, a workout territory. Take note over the next few days and notice which areas bring the most success and likeliness for chosen activities.

Ask yourself questions that may influence your chosen area. Are you more relaxed in the living room or the bedroom for reading? Are you exercising more at the gym or at home? Are there other resources around to assist you in this activity? Are you looking for quiet, space, good lighting, a territory nearby, far away?

If you notice that your current space for a specific activity is causing less productivity and likeliness of habit action, then find a new space. It's likely that you may not have an ideal space. If we do not have an ideal space, we must create one.

Maybe that means joining a gym to increase productivity and influence, as it's better than your garage gym. Or it means taking a long drive to work to listen to more of your audiobook. Perhaps it is timing and requires waking up earlier to get a meditation in or spending time at school after classes to finish projects and homework. Assess these issues and adjust; discover what works for you.

Set yourself up for success. Put your habits first. Design daily routines, organize rooms, relocate, or do anything else you believe will help you along the way to success.

Now, let's continue.

Okay, let's see: Forethought, check. Prompts, check. Now, it's time for habit execution. At first glance, this seems self-explanatory. While the actual act of executing habits is relatively straightforward, to properly structure our new habits, we must add a *before and after action.*

BEFORE: IDENTIFY TRIGGERS

We should identify triggers for new habits. To create and keep new habits, we need structure. This is where triggers come into play. Essentially, we need something to initiate our habits.

Triggers are cues that our new habits can attach to. They are what sparks our new habits into action, thus making them part of the routine. Triggers sound something like this: "When that happens, then I'll respond with this," or "When I see that, I'll do this."

These triggers are part of the routines in our lives right now. An example of a common trigger is this: Every time we wake up (the trigger), we then go for coffee (the habit). Or when we notice it's time for bed (the trigger), we brush our teeth (the habit). You see, we already have existing routines that trigger specific habits. And, if we're mindful, we can add new habits that will follow new or existing triggers.

For example, if you're looking to practice gratitude more, set up a trigger to allow you to make this habit more frequent. Try setting a reminder or an alarm on your phone to prompt you to act. Whenever you see the reminder on your phone, that's your trigger.

You could set the reminder or alarm to say "Gratitude." Set it to alarm you three times throughout the day. When you're reminded, say, think, or write a few things you're grateful for each time.

Another example—let's say you want to stretch more often. You could leave your yoga mat rolled out right next to your bed. When you first wake up and see the yoga mat, that will trigger you to get down and stretch before you do anything else that is part of your morning routine.

Purposely set the yoga mat on the floor in an area that requires you to pass it to exit your bedroom.

Essentially, we are purposely interrupting ourselves to create new routines. We want triggers to be crystal clear as they are a major piece of the habit puzzle. So, identify or create triggers to establish structure in your overarching goal to establish and keep new habits. Once we've identified our trigger, it's time for execution. No explanation is needed here—*insert chosen habit.*

AFTER: EMOTIONAL RESPONSE

In an interview with *Time* magazine, BJ Fogg kept it simple: "emotions create habits."[2] Habits can form fast if there's a positive emotion tied to the new behavior. If we're able to associate good experiences with specific habits, it sparks interest and allows for more effortless habit execution.

It's all about creating feelings of success internally. When we make positive reinforcement around a particular habit, we're more drawn to performing the habit. Thankfully, as humans, we can intentionally create such a feeling.

The point is to reward yourself for actually completing a habit so that this habit will become more attractive to act on and, overall, more automatic. Believe it or not, when purposely adding a positive emotional response after a habit, you're utilizing your brain's reward system.[3]

You see, the brain releases dopamine when rewarded, and as a result, the brain will rewire. Your brain will notice the feelings of success associated with a habit.[4] We are then more likely to engage in this habit again and again to obtain another similar positive emotional response.

There are endless ways we can respond and reward ourselves. It doesn't matter how you do it; as long as it brings you sincere feelings of success, that's all you need. It could even be something as minor as cracking a smile or patting yourself on the back.

Try different responses and see which ones work best for you. Remember, we're going for authenticity, so find a response that will trigger actual feelings of success. The feeling may vary from person to person based on their preferences.

Fair warning: This reward concept may be a little tricky at first. It may be something we need to work on as it doesn't come naturally to all. Sometimes it takes practice, so keep going.

For timing, you must reward yourself directly after the habit to tie the emotion to said habit. Having a celebratory dinner two hours after hitting the gym will not work. The reward must be received *immediately* after the habit so that the two are associated with each other.

The reward you choose for yourself may be obvious or concealed. It could be something significant like a dance or something minimal like a quiet positive comment to yourself. It's whatever works best for you at that particular moment.

I'd recommend choosing both an obvious and concealed response. If your response is to clap and cheer loudly for yourself, you probably wouldn't want to do this in a quiet public area (at least, I hope you wouldn't). You get the point.

Now, *let's review.*

There are three essential pieces to the puzzle regarding habit execution: the *before-action*, the *habit itself*, and the *after-action*. This three-piece process will allow for habits to stick—without them, our structure may be too loose and fall flat over time. So, stay with this system! Utilize these ideas to assist you on your habit-building journey.

No more bullshit habits. Eliminate the ones that sound good in theory but lack structure. You know, New Year's resolutions or the habits that are solely fueled by motivation for a mere three weeks.

Ditch the habits you take on because they "look good" or seem like something you "should do." Release this concept entirely and create the habits you truly want. Put some power behind these ideas. Stop half-assing it. Drop your willy-nilly approach—you need a real game plan.

Write down your specific goals, set reasonable expectations, make sure your habit is accessible, organize for ideal habit territory, identify triggers, perform your habit, and create feelings of success. These are all vital ingredients that make up a recipe for success in the kitchen of habit building.

CHAPTER 17: LIGHTS, CAMERA, ACTION

The concepts and tactics we've explored in this book are practical. If they weren't, I wouldn't have spent all of this time putting them into words for you to review and apply. Evidently, these concepts and tactics have withstood the test of time and are praised by experts; they've also been helpful in my own life.

They may not all work for you—and that's totally fine. If it's any consolation, meditation didn't click for me until I was about 22 years old. Now, it's my go-to tactic when I'm looking to de-stress and gain clarity.

What I'm saying is, try them all. Give each one an honest attempt with an open mind. See which ones work for you. You must find your go-to's and understand which concepts and tactics will put you on a clear path to success and bring you closer to your vision.

Look, I'll keep this short and sweet. Please note, this is vital to the success of your vision, so I'll make it crystal clear:

Nothing in this book will mean a thing if you're not taking action and directly applying these concepts and tactics.

Without action, potential opportunities will pass by, old habits will remain in place, and your vision will stay just a vision. You can spend all the time in the world sitting around thinking about these concepts and tactics, but unless you're willing to get up and put in the work, absolutely nothing will come of it.

Action is the only thing between where we are and where we want to be.

I know that taking action can be scary. It means leaving your comfort zone for uncharted territory that may or may not be what you want. But, if you never try, how will you know?

Regret is nothing to mess with. In life, there is no reset button. Imagine this: You're approaching your final days and you reflect on your life. You realize that you never took that trip, never left that dead-end job, never asked that person out, never moved, never went after the things you wanted, alongside many other fizzled-out hopes and dreams.

Here's the kicker. The most upsetting part is that you'll realize that you never even tried. Unfortunately, you let your thoughts, emotions, or other people's opinions get in the way of what you truly wanted.

Now, you're done. It's time to wave those ideas goodbye. Whatever you did is set in stone, and that's what you made of your life. You will be crushed. And here's the worst part: There's nothing you can do about it. There's no time machine, no magic, no extra chances, none of that.

Kiss it goodbye.

Or, you could get off your ass and take some ACTION!

You're here, aren't you? You woke up this morning. You're reading this book right now. So, let's go! Give it your best shot. Even if your effort were a complete train wreck, at least you would have the satisfaction of knowing you gave it everything you had.

Ask yourself: Would I rather try and fail than never know at all?

Realize that we are actually living miracles. We are human beings with a mind-boggling slim chance of even being born. What was that number again? One in $10^{2,685,000}$, right?

Consider the number of people born and the number of the potential others who missed out on this opportunity called life. It's incredible to be here in the first place. Given the circumstances, I think it's safe to say that maximizing our time would be in good taste. Wouldn't you?

So, give it your all. We are here on this planet—once. Spend your time wisely and manage your priorities. Understand the magnitude of this experience. Take that realization and maximize your time by living according to YOU. Disregard any pre-cut paths or blueprints from others on how you should live your life. Do what works for you.

Throughout your own experiences in life, you will encounter others who may have other ideal ways of living, whether it's from close friends, family, philosophers, etc. Consider them, learn from them, but don't adopt these principles if they don't align with you personally.

Draw from your OWN experiences to decide for yourself what works and what doesn't.

If you're looking to live a fulfilled life, you must live on your own terms. Now, living on your own terms doesn't mean that everything works out in your favor, everything always goes your way, or everything is lovely all of the time. It means you're constantly being your authentic self, no matter what. You're reacting to the circumstances in life the way you wish to. You're not falling in line with what others do and think because you're "supposed to."

It's not the perfect execution and flawless experiences in your life that leave you feeling fulfilled; it's the satisfaction of taking your own path. Looking back, you won't be satisfied if you realize that you lived a life based on what others thought, felt, or said. Fulfillment will come from following your own path and pursuing the goals YOU believe are most important. That's what living on your own terms looks like.

Make yourself a priority. It's not selfish to chase what you want in life. Doing things of no interest to you to fall in line with others is self-deprivation. Other people's expectations and opinions are none of your business—so treat them as such.

Again, I know taking action can be scary. But regret is undoubtedly more dreadful.

Don't be afraid to fail. Fear not trying, not knowing, of going your whole life wondering and asking yourself, What if? Failure is not the opposite of success; it's a step in the process toward success.

The core message: *action is the way*, so go for it.

DO IT NOW

Stop waiting! Enough of telling yourself that one day you'll do something. The longer you wait, the more time passes that could be spent working toward what you actually want.

You must STOP waiting for perfect moments. If you keep waiting for things to be perfect, absolutely nothing will get done. There is no perfect. You're waiting at a red light that will never turn green.

Go! Do it now. What the hell are you waiting for? You're wasting time. Don't worry about doing something right. Just worry about doing it.

When you keep reiterating things like how you're feeling, where your mind is, or if you're doing it right, all you're doing is holding yourself back. Stop checking on yourself every two seconds—you're dragging things out.

Stop worrying about how you're doing. Just put your head down and put in the work. And when you look up, you will notice how much progress you've made. If you're spending half of your time evaluating where you're at instead of continuing to march forward, you're delaying your progress.

Again, things don't need to be perfect. *Perfection isn't real*; this mindset is keeping you in a cycle, running on a figurative hamster wheel. It stops you from taking action, as you're ruminating, waiting for that imaginary green light.

Let go and execute despite not having ideal conditions. Just get started.

While planning is a crucial part of execution, taking too long may result in lost time. You can start whenever you want—but your plan *requires* action. We can let nothing get in the way of this action, not even ourselves.

Our fleeting thoughts and emotions are not always aligned with our goals—which delays our actions. Some days we may feel doubtful, fearful, anxious, or worried while on our journey. While it's wise to note our current standpoint once in a while, we must not fall to the wayside by giving into our thoughts and emotions.

Remember, your thoughts and emotions are ever-changing. They are temporary experiences. Never forget that your true beliefs and goals are more important than your temporary emotions. Run toward these goals unfazed.

While in pursuit, don't let temporary emotions get in the way. You know what's important or worth tending to and what's not.

You need to trust yourself in these doubtful moments. Be true to yourself, no matter what. Identify what is important and stick with it.

Stop questioning yourself. Stop with the constant check-ins and keep moving forward. You'll second guess yourself and spend so much time doing so you will gravitate toward this idea unconsciously. Don't let these worries beat you. Be intuitive. *You know what's right.*

We must continue forward and leave behind this stagnant nonsense. Time to level up. Stop replaying the narrative that tells us we're stuck on level whatever, and we can't get past it. Sure you can. With a little can-do attitude, you can do anything you want.

Quit waiting until you are "ready." No more imaginary start dates in your head. What pivotal moments are you waiting for to assure yourself you're prepared by then, whenever "then" is? Decide what you want to do and go for it. Stop making excuses!

NO MORE EXCUSES

No more excuses. Tired? Drink a coffee. Is it too hard? Start small. Don't know how? Learn. Too afraid? Then do it, afraid. Don't have enough time? Make the time.

Honestly, if you put in half as much effort toward creating your vision as you do making excuses, you would likely be at the halfway mark right now. Each excuse you formulate is a step backward, deeper into the comfort zone. In all honesty, it comes down to priorities.

If you're "wanting" to work out more often, but your excuse is that work is getting overwhelming, this indicates that work is a higher priority than working out. And for most people, this is the case. My problem isn't with you choosing your livelihood over your exercise routine, it's with you lying to yourself.

Look, excuses are for those who don't want it bad enough. And that's the truth.

There, I said it. Sorry, not sorry. If you're saying you want to do something and don't act on it, it is a clear sign that it's not on your list of priorities.

Why would you choose work over exercise? Well, maybe you have a family, and your job is crucial to support the current lifestyle of your family. You feel responsible for them, which is a valid reason for doing what you're doing. No wonder work is on the high-priority list.

But don't mope around constantly complaining that you don't have enough time to do what you want. You signed up for that—that's on you. You made the decisions to get there. Did you wake up one day with a spouse, a family, and a busy job, then decide to continue forward like it was normal? No, you didn't.

With priorities, you decide what's on that list—and in what order. Sure, perhaps other people are counting on you, whether it's work-related, family-related, or whatever it is. But, ask yourself a question:

Would you choose the new priority you want so "badly" over this existing or top priority? Even deeper, would you choose the new priority you want over the outcome or underlying result that derives from this existing or top priority? Let's find out.

For example, let's say you want to spend more time hiking on the weekends. It's one of the old go-to activities you haven't been able to do in recent years because of the chaotic lifestyle that comes with being a parent. As friendlier weather approaches, you may claim this is the year you want to get back into it.

Ironically, this is the same year your son wants to play baseball, your daughter takes up art classes on the weekends, and your spouse gets a new puppy. With some surface-level thinking, you may think to yourself: Sure, this is great and all, but what about me? I've gotta live too.

While that statement is entirely true and worth considering, as you need to have your own life, it's not that simple. Remember, this is something you signed up for when you had a family. This doesn't mean you can't find time to do what you want, although it may require more effort than before you had a family.

Now spending the day hiking in the great outdoors may sound a little more appealing than driving two kids around in the ugly minivan you hate so much. But let's dive a little deeper.

Let's consider the questions above once again with the provided scenario, would you choose this *new priority* you want so badly over the existing or top priority? Again, on the surface, maybe you would. But what about the outcomes or underlying results that derive from the existing or top priority?

"Now, what are you asking, exactly?"

Do the outcomes or underlying results that derive from going on a few Saturday afternoon hikes outweigh the outcomes or underlying results that derive from tending to your family?

More specifically, does your desire to exercise, spend time outdoors, and have some "you" time override your desire to foster your family, teach your children, and spend time with your spouse?

If the answer is yes, then it looks like it's time to rearrange your priorities and spend more time tending to this new priority. If the answer is no, then you're doing the right thing. Remember, this is something you're consciously choosing or something you metaphorically or maybe literally "signed up for."

Don't fret. If you're still feeling ambitious and want to take on these new priorities regardless, then it's a matter of time management and priority swapping. Adjust your list and schedule—there is a way for you to explore avenues to allow for these new priorities to come into play.

Look, I'll level with you. I'm not ignorant. Life happens. Things come up, and there are roadblocks. But, with things you *truly* want to do, don't tell me this, that, and all these other things you don't even really like, that you've labeled as top priorities, are holding you back from doing what you want.

A few things may justify why something cannot get done, but that list is minimal and tedious. If you're serious about doing something, you will find a way to do it, plain and simple.

And if not, well, then you must not want it bad enough.

CHAPTER 18: CLOSING TIME

Congratulations, you made it to the end of this book. Or maybe you skipped to the end. I mean, at least you opened it up. That's a start, regardless.

Before we depart, I want to shed some light on the purpose of this book. Now, it's obvious this book isn't filled with magic concepts and tactics that will bring you to a perfect life where you'll live happily ever after. It's a book with concepts and tactics scientifically backed and endorsed by remarkable and knowledgeable humans; its purpose is to help you overcome some of the bullshit in your life.

The point isn't to give you an unrealistic idea of what life is or what life should be like, or to write something that inspires you for a mere three weeks and then leaves you back at square one. Instead, it's to foster real progress toward your optimal life.

Not a life where you put a ludicrous amount of pressure on yourself to live a perfect one, but a life that you're happy with. A life that lets you look back sometimes and think to yourself, "Look how far I've come."

My goal is to point you in a positive direction and give you your first nudge. The rest is up to you.

"Well, why *should* I listen to you?"

Honestly, I'm not here to say whether you should or shouldn't.

Again, this is scientifically backed information proven to work. I'm just writing and presenting it because it's helped me in my own experiences. I'm just a guy who had some big questions and looked for some big answers. Life happened, and I'm glad it did.

When I consider my past and the problems I dealt with, regardless of how difficult they were, I feel very fortunate to have learned from these experiences, and I hope to pass some wisdom on to you.

I wrote this book for a variety of reasons, but mainly for this one: to help others. If I could go back in time, this is the book I would hand to my past self. It undoubtedly would've saved me some time.

And that, my friend, is my plan for you.

The plan is for you to take these concepts and tactics and utilize them. Perhaps they'll save you some time, worry, or suffering. Ideally, you will pass these lessons to others and help them as well. Maybe you recall the positive ripple effect? Ah, yes, it's all aligning.

Do you see where I'm going with this?

HELP EACH OTHER

Life can be a little crazy occasionally. It's filled with anxious moments, sad situations, and honestly, sometimes, complete bullshit. Life's not fair. It has never been, and it never will be.

But as we progress through life, we're given opportunities to learn. We can learn from our mistakes, peers, parents, experiences, and, literally, everything else. As we maneuver through life, we accumulate life lessons that can be distributed from one person to the next.

These life lessons, which we're so fortunate to collect, act like pieces of armor.

That's right—armor.

Each lesson we receive is like an added piece of protection; these lessons are great bits of insight and information that prepare us for future situations. Thankfully, we can pass these pieces of armor (lessons) around to friends, family, and others to protect them as well. The only catch is that the other person must be *willing* to receive this armor.

And as we accumulate these life lessons, it's imperative to share said lessons with one another.

You see, we're all knights, walking into this battle called life. It has all the elements of a great story: hardships, loss, drama, sadness, fear, anger, resentment, disappointments, worries, and borderline insane situations and experiences.

Luckily, in its opposition, we're exposed to other elements like success, victory, love, happiness, hope, beauty, courage, glory, strength, friendships, and many other sublime situations and experiences.

Before I get too far off track, here's the bottom line: life is filled with adversity. The duality of life's highs and lows can be overwhelming and leave us feeling like we're being pulled in multiple directions. We are all going through something, and we are all learning. This includes myself; I'm in it with you.

Look, I'm only human, so I don't have all the answers. No one does. But evidently, we all have *some* answers. So, why wouldn't we take the time to share this information with other people? Perhaps it will help save them some time, worry, or suffering. Essentially, what I'm looking to emphasize in this section is this: *share your life lessons with others.*

Empower others by sharing the valuable information you possess with them and help these other people arm themselves for life. By sharing these life lessons you've obtained through your own experiences, you will initiate a positive ripple effect. Anytime you commence a positive ripple effect, you contribute some good to the universe that will transcend your imagination.

There's no telling how far and wide the impact of your actions will go—it's simply a mystery. Furthermore, we should be mindful of our actions and the ripple effects we create. We should intentionally try to create positive experiences for others and ourselves. With that said, make it a priority to share the helpful pieces of information you have stored. Be of service to others and help them learn and live in a more convenient way.

GET BUSY

While we cannot live perfect lives, we can certainly live optimal ones. Although, moving closer to the vision we've created for our optimal life is not a walk in the park. There will be obstacles. There will be difficulties. There will be failures.

You will transition into a new lifestyle when you utilize the concepts and tactics in this book. Again, it's not easy, but it will be worth it. Don't give in to the adversity that comes along with this process. You are stronger than that. Proceed toward your optimal life without resistance—just persistence and perseverance. Confront these issues head-on and be the person you know you can be.

Build the vision. See it, feel it, and believe it. *Know* that it's possible. And once that's done, take action. Put these ideas to work and let the grind begin. Continue pushing, no matter what.

If there's a problem, solve it. If there's an obstacle, go around it. If you fall, get back up. Don't let *anything* get in your way.

Above all, throughout your journey, believe in yourself and continue to take action. Life's not going to change itself, so get going. And that's the key right there—*to get going.*

There's no time to lose. Get busy.

You got this.

With love,
Nick

ACKNOWLEDGEMENTS

Throughout the research and writing of *Build the Vision: Advance Toward Your Optimal Life*, I received an incredible amount of help and support from others. Thank you to those who have assisted me on this beautiful journey. This book wouldn't be what it is without all of you.

First, thank you, Dr. D. Ivan Young, MCC, NBC-HWC, CPDC, for your extreme generosity in writing the foreword for this book. I appreciate the time and wisdom that you've passed to me and am delighted for the opportunity to share this information with others. Your encouragement throughout this process was like no other.

Website: https://drdivanyoung.com/

Next, thank you to Dr. Chelsea Shields, PhD, for the stimulating conversations and stellar book recommendations. It was a privilege to chat about social health with you and to discuss helpful strategies I may now enjoyably share with others. In addition, you have deepened my understanding of the importance of companionship. I am beyond grateful for the insight and lessons you've provided and look forward to implementing such things into my own life.

Thank you, Sally Kempton, for our informative and insightful conversations. Your wisdom shines bright. I appreciate your kindness and willingness to share this information with me. My perspective on detachment has broadened dramatically because of our connection. Thank you.

Website: https://www.sallykempton.com/

And finally, thank you, Mark Daniello, for the wonderful artwork that graciously covers the front of this book. Your art has always inspired me, and I am thrilled to share this project to showcase yet another extraordinary piece of your work. Words cannot describe how amazing that is to me. Don't ever stop creating.

AUTHOR'S NOTE

Thank you for taking this journey with me. Your personal journey toward your optimal life is an exciting voyage. I'd like to take this time to note that while self-help can surely be beneficial, there's nothing wrong with getting professional help when it's necessary. Self-help isn't everything, and as humans, we can't do everything alone. I've spent plenty of hours in therapy and it has truly worked wonders. There are many resources at hand for you to use (e.g., BetterHelp online therapy). Use them if need be and become the person YOU KNOW you can be. Good luck!

NOTES

Foreword

1)   Dr. D. Ivan Young. Foreword to *Build the Vision: Advance Toward Your Optimal Life*. 2022.

Expectations

1)   quoteresearch, Author, and Theodore Roosevelt. "Comparison Is the Thief of Joy." Quote Investigator, February 7, 2021. https://quoteinvestigator.com/2021/02/06/thief-of-joy/.

2)   Ruiz, Miguel, Janet Mills, and Miguel Ruiz. *The Four Agreements*. Thorndike, Me.: Center Point Pub., 2008.

3)   Ibid.

Law of Attraction

1)   Montana, Cate. "The Illusion of Reality: Scientists Find Proof That Everything Is Energy." Conscious Lifestyle Magazine, April 25, 2019. https://www.consciouslifestylemag.com/everything-is-energy-illusion-reality/.

2)   Meah, Asad. "The Law of Vibration from Bob Proctor." AwakenTheGreatnessWithin, September 23, 2017. https://www.awakenthegreatnesswithin.com/the-law-of-vibration-from-bob-proctor/.

3)   "How the Law of Attraction Works." Proctor Gallagher Institute, January 16, 2018. https://www.proctorgallagherinstitute.com/6809/how-the-law-of-

attraction-works.

4)   Stanborough, Rebecca Joy. "What Is Vibrational Energy? Definition, Benefits & More." Healthline. Healthline Media, November 13, 2020. https://www.healthline.com/health/vibrational-energy.

5)   Mayer, Gil. "Subconscious Mind – How to Unlock and Use Its Power." Thrive, March 15, 2018. https://thriveglobal.com/stories/subconscious-mind-how-to-unlock-and-use-its-power/#:~:text=The%20subconscious%20mind%20is%20a,is%20also%20your%20guidance%20system.

6)   "How Your Mind Works." Proctor Gallagher Institute, March 6, 2018. https://www.proctorgallagherinstitute.com/25593/how-your-mind-works.

7)   McGinley, Karson. "How to Raise Your Emotional & Spiritual Vibration." Chopra. Chopra, May 11, 2022. https://chopra.com/articles/a-complete-guide-to-raise-your-vibration.

8)   Einzelganger. "The Backwards Law." Einzelgänger, February 24, 2022. https://einzelganger.co/the-backwards-law/.

Intuition

1)   Davenport, Matt. "Revealing the Logic of the Body's 'Second Brain'." MSUToday, October 1, 2021. https://msutoday.msu.edu/news/2021/logic-of-the-second-brain.

2)   Earth, BBC. "Meet Your Second Brain." Magzter. Magzter, March 2017.

https://www.magzter.com/stories/5447/209573/58bf7d95bbeef.

3)   "Vagus Nerve." Physiopedia. Accessed May 10, 2022.
https://www.physio-pedia.com/Vagus_Nerve.

4)   Vobora, David, and TEDx Talks. "Trust Your Gut | David
Vobora | TEDxSMU." YouTube. YouTube, December 9, 2016.
https://www.youtube.com/watch?v=faGUQ06fR1Y.

5)   Doraisamy, Jerome. "Humans Have Two Brains, and They're
Both Important." Wellness Daily, November 1, 2018.
https://www.wellnessdaily.com.au/health/humans-have-two-brains-
and-theyre-both-important.

Detachment

1)   Shetty, Jay. *Think like a Monk*. New York: Simon & Schuster,
2020.

2)   "Why Detached Love Is Infinite & Pure - Jay Shetty Genius."
Jay Shetty Genius, March 7, 2022.
https://jayshettygenius.com/blog/why-detached-love-is-infinite-and-
pure-
love/#:~:text=As%20the%20Bhagavad%20Gita%20teaches,loved%20just
%20as%20you%20are.

3)   Shetty, Jay. *Think Like a Monk*. New York: Simon & Schuster,
2020.

4)   Kempton, Sally. "Just Let Go." Sally Kempton, August 28,
2020. https://www.sallykempton.com/just-let-go/.

5)   Spector, Dina, and Ali Binazir. "The Odds of You Being Alive Are Incredibly Small." Business Insider. Business Insider, June 11, 2012. https://www.businessinsider.com/infographic-the-odds-of-being-alive-2012-6.

6)   Ibid.

Autosuggestion and Affirmations

1)   "Émile Coué." Encyclopædia Britannica. Encyclopædia Britannica, inc. Accessed May 12, 2022. https://www.britannica.com/biography/Emile-Coue.

2)   Walker, Marilyn. "Emile Coue: Biography of Famous French Psychologist." CBT, February 7, 2022. https://www.cbtcognitivebehavioraltherapy.com/emile-coue-biography/.

3)   Ibid.

4)   Ibid.

5)   Robertson, Donald. "Émile Coué's Method of 'Conscious Autosuggestion'." The UK College of Hypnosis and Hypnotherapy - Hypnotherapy Training Courses, July 7, 2021. https://www.ukhypnosis.com/2009/06/17/emile-coues-method-of-conscious-autosuggestion/.

6)   Émile Coué Quote." Lib Quotes. Accessed May 12, 2022. https://libquotes.com/%C3%A9mile-cou%C3%A9/quote/lbg0e6d.

7)   "Emile Coue: Self Mastery through Conscious Autosuggestion

& the Practice of Autosuggestion (Including the Study of the Emile Coue's Method & Biography of the Author)." Google Books. Google. Accessed May 12, 2022. https://books.google.com/books?id=33VODwAAQBAJ&pg=PT13&lpg=PT13&dq=The%2Binfluence%2Bof%2Bthe%2Bimagination%2Bupon%2Bthe%2Bmoral%2Band%2Bphysical%2Bbeing%2Bof%2Bmankind%2Bemile%2Bcoue&source=bl&ots=fU3ULlrcKL&sig=ACfU3U2RJckZcphcxpAN0siMe8WDLs-2uA&hl=en&sa=X&ved=2ahUKEwjpldThrtr3AhUNU98KHSJND-oQ6AF6BAgZEAM#v=onepage&q&f=false.

8)   Cuncic, Arlin. "What Happens to Your Body When You're Thinking?" Verywell Mind. Verywell Mind, July 17, 2019. https://www.verywellmind.com/what-happens-when-you-think-4688619.

9)   Cascio, Christopher N, Matthew Brook O'Donnell, Francis J Tinney, Matthew D Lieberman, Shelley E Taylor, Victor J Strecher, and Emily B Falk. "Self-Affirmation Activates Brain Systems Associated with Self-Related Processing and Reward and Is Reinforced by Future Orientation." Social cognitive and affective neuroscience. Oxford University Press, April 2016. https://www.ncbi.nlm.nih.gov/pmc/articles/PMC4814782/.

10)   Coué, Émile. "Self Mastery through Conscious Autosuggestion." Google Books. Google. Accessed May 16, 2022. https://books.google.com/books?id=epJi6BAo0PYC&printsec=frontcover&source=gbs_ge_summary_r&cad=0#v=onepage&q=impossible&f=false.

11)   Ibid.

12)   Ibid.

13)   Ibid.

14)   Ibid.

15)   Karefilakis, Maria. "The Conscious and Subconscious Mind."
Kare Psychology, February 22, 2019.
https://karepsychology.com.au/the-conscious-and-subconscious-mind/.

Meditation

1)   McGreevey, Sue. "Eight Weeks to a Better Brain." Harvard
Gazette. Harvard Gazette, September 12, 2019.
https://news.harvard.edu/gazette/story/2011/01/eight-weeks-to-a-
better-
brain/#:~:text=In%20a%20study%20that%20will,in%20the%20brain's%
20gray%20matter.

2)   Ibid.

3)   Ibid.

4)   Ibid.

5)   Ibid.

6)   MassGeneralNews. "Mindfulness Meditation Training
Changes Brain Structure in 8 Weeks." EurekAlert! Accessed May 11,
2022. https://www.eurekalert.org/news-releases/628286.

7) Comninos, Andreas. "Negative Thinking: Important Things Your Brain Doesn't Know." Mindfulness & Clinical Psychology Solutions, April 7, 2022. https://mi-psych.com.au/what-your-brain-doesnt-know/.

8) Comninos, Andreas. "Emotion Regulation Essentials: Your Brain's Threat System." Mindfulness & Clinical Psychology Solutions, April 7, 2022. https://mi-psych.com.au/your-brains-threat-system/.

Gratitude

1) "Global Wash Fast Facts." Centers for Disease Control and Prevention. Centers for Disease Control and Prevention, December 8, 2021.
https://www.cdc.gov/healthywater/global/wash_statistics.html#:~:text=Access%20to%20Clean%20Water%2C%20Sanitation%2C%20and%20Hygiene&text=The%20latest%20published%20information%20on,have%20safe%20water%20to%20drink.

2) "Giving Thanks Can Make You Happier." Harvard Health, August 14, 2021. https://www.health.harvard.edu/healthbeat/giving-thanks-can-make-you-happier.

Physical Wellness

1) "Nutrition, Physical Activity, and Obesity." Nutrition, Physical Activity, and Obesity | Healthy People 2020. Accessed June 14, 2022. https://www.healthypeople.gov/2020/leading-health-indicators/2020-lhi-topics/Nutrition-Physical-Activity-and-Obesity.

Fitness

1) "Benefits of Exercise." MedlinePlus. U.S. National Library of Medicine. Accessed June 14, 2022.

https://medlineplus.gov/benefitsofexercise.html.

2)   Bruce, Debra Fulghum. "Exercise and Depression: Endorphins, Reducing Stress, and More." WebMD. WebMD. Accessed June 14, 2022. https://www.webmd.com/depression/guide/exercise-depression.

3)   "Working out Boosts Brain Health." American Psychological Association. American Psychological Association, 2020. https://www.apa.org/topics/exercise-fitness/stress#:~:text=Research%20shows%20that%20while%20exercise,causes%20a%20rush%20of%20endorphins.

4)   "How Exercise Affects Sleep." Sleep.org, January 28, 2022. https://www.sleep.org/how-sleep-works/exercise-affects-sleep/.

Nutrition

1)   "Benefits of Healthy Eating." Centers for Disease Control and Prevention. Centers for Disease Control and Prevention, May 16, 2021. https://www.cdc.gov/nutrition/resources-publications/benefits-of-healthy-eating.html.

2)   Kubala, Jillian. "11 High Cholesterol Foods – Which to Eat, Which to Avoid." Healthline. Healthline Media, January 13, 2022. https://www.healthline.com/nutrition/high-cholesterol-foods#:~:text=Fried%20foods%2C%20such%20as%20deep,many%20other%20ways%20(%2025%20).

3)   "Food & Your Mood: How Food Affects Mental Health – Aetna: Foods That Help Your Brain Health." Aetna. Accessed June 13, 2022. https://www.aetna.com/health-guide/food-affects-mental-health.html#:~:text=Eating%20healthy%20food%20promotes%20the,ca

use%20inflammation%20that%20hampers%20production.

4)   Robertson, Ruairi. "Why Bifidobacteria Are So Good for You." Healthline. Healthline Media, July 25, 2017. https://www.healthline.com/nutrition/why-bifidobacteria-are-good#TOC_TITLE_HDR_5.

5)   "Family Physician Shares Signs of Poor Gut Health." Piedmont Healthcare. Accessed June 13, 2022. https://www.piedmont.org/living-better/signs-of-poor-gut-health.

6)   Rockwood, Kate. "The Best (and Worst) Foods for Your Gut." Rally Health, 2020. https://www.rallyhealth.com/food/the-best-and-worst-foods-for-your-gut.

7)   "Food & Your Mood: How Food Affects Mental Health – Aetna: Foods That Help Your Brain Health." Aetna. Accessed June 14, 2022. https://www.aetna.com/health-guide/food-affects-mental-health.html.

Sleep

1)   "Sleep Matters: The Impact of Sleep on Health and Wellbeing." Mental Health Foundation, February 11, 2020. https://www.mentalhealth.org.uk/publications/sleep-report.

2)   "The Benefits of Getting a Full Night's Sleep." SCL Health. Accessed June 13, 2022. https://www.sclhealth.org/blog/2018/09/the-benefits-of-getting-a-full-night-sleep/.

3)   Calveiro, Lissette. "Studies Show Sleep Deprivation Performance Is Similar to Being under the Influence of Alcohol."

HuffPost. HuffPost, December 7, 2017.
https://www.huffpost.com/entry/studies-show-sleep-deprivation-
performance-is-similar-to-being-under-the-influence-of-
alcohol_b_9562992.

4)   "Blue Light Exposed." Blue Light Exposed. Accessed June 13,
2022. http://www.bluelightexposed.com/#where-is-the-increased-
exposure-to-blue-light-coming-from.

5)   "How Blue Light Affects Sleep." Sleep Foundation, April 12,
2022. https://www.sleepfoundation.org/bedroom-environment/blue-
light#:~:text=Blue%20light%20stimulates%20parts%20of,sleep%20after
%20the%20sun%20sets.

6)   "The Best Temperature for Sleep: Advice & Tips." Sleep
Foundation, March 11, 2022.
https://www.sleepfoundation.org/bedroom-environment/best-
temperature-for-sleep.

Journaling
1)   Grothaus, Michael, and Maud Purcell. "Why Journaling Is
Good for Your Health (and 8 Tips to Get Better)." Fast Company. Fast
Company, January 29, 2015.
https://www.fastcompany.com/3041487/8-tips-to-more-effective-
journaling-for-health.

2)   Ibid.

Positivity
1)   Long, Jamie, and Samara Quintero. "Toxic Positivity: The Dark
Side of Positive Vibes." The Psychology Group Fort Lauderdale, March

29, 2022. https://thepsychologygroup.com/toxic-positivity/.

Social Wellness
1)   "Social Wellness Is the Key to a Healthy Lifestyle." Advantage Care Health Center, July 13, 2018. https://advantagecaredtc.org/social-wellness/.

Social Health
1)   Lieberman, Matthew D. *Social: Why Our Brains Are Wired to Connect.* Oxford: Oxford Univ. Press, 2015.

2)   George, Tammy. "What Is Social Health? Definitions, Examples and Tips on Improving Your Social Wellness." HIF. Accessed June 7, 2022. https://blog.hif.com.au/mental-health/what-is-social-health-definitions-examples-and-tips-on-improving-your-social-wellness.

3)   Eisenberger, Naomi I. "The Neural Bases of Social Pain: Evidence for Shared Representations with Physical Pain." Psychosomatic medicine. U.S. National Library of Medicine, 2012. https://www.ncbi.nlm.nih.gov/pmc/articles/PMC3273616/.

4)   Graham, Sarah. "Brain's Own Pain Relievers at Work in Placebo Effect, Study Suggests." Scientific American. Scientific American, August 24, 2005. https://www.scientificamerican.com/article/brains-own-pain-relievers/#:~:text=According%20to%20a%20report%20published,activity%20of%20their%20endorphin%20system.

5)   Williams, Vivien. "Mayo Clinic Minute: The Benefits of Being Socially Connected - Mayo Clinic News Network." Mayo Clinic. Mayo

Foundation for Medical Education and Research, March 4, 2022.
https://newsnetwork.mayoclinic.org/discussion/mayo-clinic-minute-the-benefits-of-being-socially-connected/.

6)   García Héctor, and Francesc Miralles. *Ikigai*. Kbh.: People'sPress, 2017.

7)   McGregor, Jena. "This Former Surgeon General Says There's a 'Loneliness Epidemic' and Work Is Partly to Blame." The Washington Post. WP Company, December 5, 2021.
https://www.washingtonpost.com/news/on-leadership/wp/2017/10/04/this-former-surgeon-general-says-theres-a-loneliness-epidemic-and-work-is-partly-to-blame/.

8)   TEDxTalks. "How's Your Social Health? Let's Test It. | Dr. Chelsea Shields | Tedxsaltlakecity." YouTube. YouTube, December 18, 2020. https://www.youtube.com/watch?v=bfCZBXQYSlw&t=170s.

Building Habits
1)   Clear, James. *Atomic Habits: An Easy & Proven Way to Build Good Habits & Break Bad Ones*. New York: Avery, an imprint of Penguin Random House, 2018.

2)   Fogg, BJ. "Better Control Emotions Will Help You Create Better Habits." Time. Time, December 30, 2019.
https://time.com/5756833/better-control-emotions-better-habits/.

3)   Ibid.

4)   Ibid.

Lights, Camera, Action

1)   Spector, Dina, and Ali Binazir. "The Odds of You Being Alive Are Incredibly Small." Business Insider. Business Insider, June 11, 2012. https://www.businessinsider.com/infographic-the-odds-of-being-alive-2012-6.